A Chautauquan Searches Paris
for the Best Tarte au Citron

A Chautauquan Searches Paris for the Best Tarte au Citron

Herbert H. Keyser, M.D.

A KEYGARD BOOK

A KEYGARD BOOK

7887 Broadway, Suite 506

San Antonio, TX 78209

E-mail: Bhkeyser@aol.com

ISBN 0-9767086-0-4

Composition, Printing, and Binding:
Sheridan Books, Inc., Ann Arbor, Michigan

Cover design by Susan Miller

To Barbara

Whose help on this book was crucial to making it possible!

Whose love in my life makes living special!!!

Other books by author:

WOMEN UNDER THE KNIFE

PRESCRIPTION FOR DISASTER: Health Care in America

TWO DRIFTERS . . . OFF TO SEE THE WORLD

Contents

Acknowledgments

How could a cookbook written by a physician possibly be created without acknowledgments? Certainly this book could not even have started were it not for the amazing generosity of fourteen of the most famous pastry chefs in Paris. Those stars of the patisserie world, each one named and interviewed in his separate chapter, were generous to me beyond all expectations. They took me into their kitchens, taught me how to make their individual recipes for lemon tarts and wined and dined me in the process. I cannot thank them enough.

At the Chautauqua Institution the enthusiasm and support for this project has been unsparing. Michael P. Sullivan and David Williams of the Administration were continuously supportive. The Chautauquan Daily provided invaluable assistance with the foreword; and photographers Roger J. Coda and Marie Ho did the photography for the cover and title pages.

Anne Landgraf and Lisa Beck provided all the expertise I did not have in the composition of a cookbook, while Susan Miller was responsible for the layout of the cover. Rebecca Humrich lead me through all the business aspects of assembling the book.

My son Christopher Keyser tried to clean up all my grammatical mistakes, but some tasks are just too overwhelming. I cannot thank him sufficiently for all his efforts.

Last, but definitely not least, is my dear wife Barbara. At the significant risk of destroying her figure by consuming multiple lemon tarts for weeks on end in Paris, she ate her way through this divine experience. Back home, as I attempted to duplicate each of the recipes, she was my taste-tester. It took a lot of bravery to sample my initial efforts, but she was a trooper. Finally, her editing eliminated many errors in my earlier drafts. I could not have done this without her.

Foreword

Herb and Barbara Keyser are long time patrons of The Left Bank Restaurant, and a few years ago Dr. Keyser started his intensive research on the different ways of making Lemon Tarts with passion and focus.

He would tell us of his travels to France every time he visited and we would enjoy each episode without realizing that this book would ultimately become a reality. We were thrilled to see the completion of this finished product based on the recipes of some of the most famous pastry chefs in Paris.

I am much honored to be part of this book and happy to have helped him in his pursuit.

Vive La Tarte au Citron et Bon Appetit.
Merci,

Luc Meyer, Chef/Owner
The Left Bank Restaurant
Vail, Colorado

Chautauqua

For more than 130 years a center of learning, the arts, religion and recreation has found a home on the shores of Lake Chautauqua in western New York State. The Chautauqua Institution has prospered in a format where, for nine weeks of every summer, famous lecturers, which have included many of our country's Presidents, share varied ideas in a spirit of listening and sharing. Balanced with that is a renowned program of performance and education in the arts, including symphony, opera, theatre, ballet, the visual arts and literature. The Religion Department presents a program of ecumenical worship and interfaith lectures and is a leader in promoting understanding among the three Abrahamic traditions: Christianity, Judaism and Islam. Finally, a broad variety of physical activities are available, including golf, tennis, sailing, softball, swimming in both the lake and an indoor pool, and exercise at two state-of-the-art fitness centers. A complete children's and young adults' program and a massive adult education schedule round out this magical place.

Food traditions have not been neglected. Since 1881 a stately Victorian hotel, the Athenaeum, has held its high position overlooking the lake. Its guests stay on the American plan, taking their meals in the hotel's grand dining room. All who stay know of the tradition that calls for guests to be served two desserts following each meal.

Another time-honored tradition calls for ice cream in the evening. After concerts in the Amphitheater or performances of opera or theatre, crowds flock to the ice cream vendors, coming away with scoops stacked two and three high.

Finally, as the 21st century began, a new food tradition found its way into the tree-shaded village. Following the research that led to the publication of this book, delicious lemon tarts, or tarte au citron, were prepared and sold to raise funds for the Institution. The response was so great that today they are sold in individual portions at a booth on the grounds. They have become part of the food tradition of the Chautauqua Institution.

We hope you will enjoy reading the "A Chautauquan Searches Paris For The Best Lemon Tarts", and that you will enjoy making them and, most of all, that you will enjoy eating them here in Chautauqua.

Introduction

Some people, given the option, would begin every meal with dessert. Some people probably do. But Barbara and I follow the routine custom of having our dessert after our meal. By then we are usually quite full and not infrequently completely pass on anything sweet.

Chocolate, most likely, is the most widely used ingredient of desserts, and probably the most popular. But, although we are both fond of chocolate in small amounts, the richness of it is frequently more than we can handle after a full meal. The result is that we usually seek lighter and more refreshing choices, if we are going to have dessert at all.

Over the years fruit desserts are the ones we are most likely to try, and we narrowed down to the point where lemon tarts are our favorite. Beyond that, we believe that no better lemon tarts, i.e. tartes au citron, can be found than in France.

As a result Barbara and I decided one day to try to compile a number of very special lemon tart recipes. All of the recipes in this book came from the best we could find in Paris, where we always found the most wonderful food.

This book will cover a five week period spent tasting and testing as many tartes au citron as we could physically accomplish. It wasn't always easy, we consumed more than our share of carbohydrates, but it was always fun. The work began in the

United States as we contacted every highly regarded restaurant and patisserie in Paris. Once we established a relationship, arrangements needed to be made for tasting, obtaining a recipe and interviewing the pastry chef. We'll try to take you through the entire process, partially as a food book and partially as a travelogue through five weeks of Paris.

One of our primary concerns from the very beginning was a fear that everyone made a tarte au citron very much like everyone else. That would make the presentation of many different recipes quite worthless. We were happily surprised to find that the differences between these patissiers was immense.

Not every fine restaurant in Paris makes a tarte au citron, and some that do may not have wanted to share their recipe. We did not include any tartes for which we were unable to obtain the recipe.

Barbara and I love cooking and sharing it with our friends. We took all these recipes from these special places and then tried to duplicate them at home. We'll tell you how they came out in our own hands.

We hope you'll try these recipes and have as much success, or more, than we had when we made them. They will bring a wonderful conclusion to your meal.

So, bon voyage and bon appetit!

Helpful Hints on How to Make the Best Tarte au Citron

The French make the most delicious tartes we have ever put in our mouths. Of course, that could be said for most everything the French do in the kitchen.

When we first started on this project, a dear friend, and true French chef, who runs one of the finest French restaurants in the United States agreed to meet with us to offer some advice. His first thought about our undertaking took this form.

"My advice to you is to concentrate on your profession of delivering babies and leave the cooking and baking to me. And I will promise not to deliver any babies".

Though not in the slightest bit discouraged we found out later why he made such a suggestion. Our first attempt at baking these recipes was fraught with difficulties. That is why this chapter has been written. It is an effort to have you avoid the pitfalls we encountered and get wonderful results right off the bat.

We can absolutely guarantee that the more of these you try, the better and better you will get. You will also find that they are so easy to make you will want to serve them repeatedly both to your family and to guests.

The most encouraging thing we can tell you is that every one of the patissiers in France agreed that of all the desserts they make, tarte au citron is by far the easiest. It is also one of the most delicious and refreshing. So start yourself off by reading these general instructions, and be prepared for lemon tartes like you've never tasted before!

1. You will soon learn that of the two parts to the recipe, by far the most difficult to master is the pastry.

2. The flour I have used in all these recipes is pastry flour. I have had the best results when using King Arthur pastry flour. It can be difficult to find on the shelves, but can be ordered by mail order on-line. As an alternative all the tarts can be made with all-purpose unbleached flour which is always available.

3. Some of the patissiers prepare their pastry by hand. That is certainly an option worth trying. But, it can be time consuming, at times difficult, and may often result in a failed recipe. It is valuable to remember that these patissiers have made thousands of tarts by hand and can tell just by touch when the pastry is right.

This may be the most important paragraph in the book. Whenever it was indicated by the patissier we made the pastry by hand. For us, the results were very inconsistent. Some of the tarts were fine and others were atrocious. When we followed the exact same recipe using a food processor we were able to get results that were consistently excellent. We were unable to discern the difference between them and the best hand mixed we had made. In using the food processor we added all of the ingredients at one time, generally placing the dry items first, and liquids on top, so that the liquid would not sink to the bottom. In most cases the patissiers themselves used mechanical means rather than making the pastry by hand. So use a food processor for any of them without any qualms. BUT, WHICHEVER METHOD YOU USE, HANDLE THE PASTRY AS LITTLE AS POSSIBLE.

4. In most of the recipes the volume of dough prepared will be sufficient for two tarts. When dividing the ball of dough in half to be refrigerated, shape each half into a flattened disc. That will make the preparation much simpler when the dough is removed from the refrigerator to be rolled out.

5. In every recipe the pastry will be left wrapped in the refrigerator for a minimum of several hours. In all cases it can be left refrigerated overnight. That will enable you to do the first step, easily accomplished in about fifteen minutes, the day before. In most cases the lemon cream can be made the day before as well.

6. On the day you are actually making the tarte, DO NOT REMOVE THE PASTRY FROM THE REFRIGERATOR UNTIL IMMEDIATELY BEFORE YOU ARE GOING TO BEGIN. If it is not cold you will have difficulty in rolling and preparing it. Roll the pastry on the coolest surface you can find. A refrigerated cooled surface is the best, such as a piece of marble left in the refrigerator. But that is not absolutely necessary.

7. The instructions call for the pastry to be rolled to a thickness between ⅛ and ¼ of an inch. The thinner you get it, closer to ⅛ inch, the better your tarte will be. But it is also true that the thinner it gets, the more difficult the handling of the rolled out pastry becomes. Having the pastry well cooled, sprinkling it and the rolling pin continuously with small amounts of flour during the rolling, and completing this step QUICKLY, are a big help.

8. Though less handling is important, if, in the process of rolling, the pastry is getting soft and sticky, stop and flour it slightly more, recool it, and start all over again.

9. When the rolling is completed, place the rolling pin in the center of the rolled out pastry and gently lift half of the dough dropping it over the pin to the other half of the dough. Then lift up the rolling pin with half of the dough hanging down each side of the pin. Bring the dough to the **VERY WELL BUTTERED** rim and cookie sheet allowing the dough to be dropped over the rim with about one or more inches hanging over the portion closest to you. Then flip over the remaining dough so that the dough extends about that much over the rest of the rim as well. That means for a seven inch rim the diameter of the rolled out dough should be about ten to eleven inches.

10. When the pastry is dropped over the tarte rim and falls down onto the cookie sheet, fold the excess back against the inside of the rim. The dough pressed up against the rim can be about twice the thickness of the bottom. It is possible that some holes or defects will be seen, especially where the pastry bends up the side of the rim. Folding in the dough hanging over the outside will double up the thickness on the inside of the rim. There will be leftover pastry hanging over the top of the rim which should be sliced off with a **VERY SHARP KNIFE**. Take little pieces of the dough to be discarded and patch up the small holes.

In some of the recipes the patissiers cover the pastry with parchment paper or aluminum foil and then weigh down the pastry with metal weights or dried beans when they begin baking. We have found obtaining those supplies can be a problem and handling the equipment can be difficult. As a result we have eliminated that step in all our preparations.

In some of the recipes the chefs make fork holes in the bottom of the pastry. I found that very helpful. As a result I have replaced the use of weights on my pastry by making multiple holes in the bottom of **ALL** my tarts before starting the baking.

IT IS ABSOLUTELY CRITICAL, IN THE FIVE RECIPES IN WHICH THE LEMON CREAM IS COOKED INSIDE THE HALF DONE PASTRY SHELL (RELAIS D'AUTEUIL, LES CELEBRITES, LASSERRE, LAURENT & VIVAROIS) THAT THERE NOT BE THE SLIGHTEST HOLE OR DEFECT IN THE PASTRY, AND THAT NO FORK HOLES BE MADE BEFORE STARTING THE BAKING. IF THERE IS THE SMALLEST HOLE, THE LIQUID LEMON CREAM WHICH IS POURED INTO THE HALF-BAKED SHELL WILL LEAK THROUGH ONTO YOUR COOKIE SHEET AND RUIN THE TART. THESE ARE THE MOST DIFFICULT TO MAKE, BUT THE RESULTS ARE WELL REWARDING.

11. Use a firm flat cookie sheet. If a sturdy cookie sheet is not available, use a baking pan upside down.

12. It's a very good idea to use an oven thermometer to see how accurate your oven actually is. Preheat your oven for almost a half hour before baking, and check to see if your temperatures are calibrated accurately. It may be necessary for you to set your oven slightly higher or lower depending on how accurate your oven is. If you are using a convection oven

HERE IS A LITTLE PIECE OF ADVICE WHICH WILL NOT HELP IN THE PROCESS OF MAKING YOUR FIRST TART, BUT IT WILL GIVE YOU VALUABLE INFORMATION CONCERNING THE ACCURACY OF YOUR OVEN TEMPERATURE, AND HELP IN MAKING SUBSEQUENT ONES. AFTER YOU HAVE BAKED THE PASTRY AND COOLED IT, TURN IT UPSIDE DOWN. THERE YOU WILL SEE THE BEST PROOF, A GOLDEN BROWN COLOR. IF IT IS SEEN ON THE BOTTOM, YOUR TIMING WAS ABSOLUTELY RIGHT.

THIS APPLIES ONLY TO THE NINE RECIPES IN WHICH THE PASTRY IS BAKED SEPARATELY FROM THE CREAM.

use the same temperature but consider removing your tarte from the oven a few minutes sooner than with a conventional oven. In most of the recipes the time of baking ranges from fifteen to twenty minutes. The best gauge is the appearance of a golden brown color. If your pastry has not reached that by the time recommended, continue baking, and checking frequently so that it is not overdone or underdone. I found this to be the most common error, yielding pastry either too doughy or too hard. After several attempts you will learn what works just right for your oven.

At times with certain recipes, during the first few minutes of the baking, I have found that the dough against the inside of the rim will tend to slip down. As a result I began removing the cookie sheet from the oven at five minutes, and with a teaspoon re-pressed the dough back up against the inside of the rim. Within a matter of seconds I returned the cookie sheet to the oven to continue baking.

I also try to remember to turn the cookie sheet a full 180 degrees about halfway through baking to compensate for uneven heating in the oven.

13. Remember that baking is like chemistry. Cooking, as opposed to baking, can be much more forgiving about accuracy. Be very certain that you measure ingredients carefully. The relationships between flour and butter and eggs can be critical in the pastry. The relationship of lemon juice to eggs is especially crucial in making the lemon cream. Recipes that call for "the juice of one lemon" are frequently not accurate, as all lemons provide a different quantity of juice. That is why in all of the recipes I have stated a specific volume. The volume of the eggs should be standard as well. I always use **LARGE** eggs in my recipes.

14. Always use unsalted butter.

15. In most cases the butter should be softened to room temperature. That is best accomplished by leaving it out for a while before starting to mix. If one neglects to remove the butter from the refrigerator an alternate softening method is to slice the butter into smaller pieces before adding it.

16. Many of the recipes call for almond powder as an ingredient. Than can be difficult to find. Fine food stores generally carry it in there bulk food departments. It is actually nothing more than very finely ground almonds. In one location we found that we could only find pecan powder which served the purpose quite well. The only difference is that almonds apparently can be ground to a finer texture than

pecans. It is also true that one **CAN** eliminate that ingredient from the recipe without a major problem.

17. Several recipes call for gelatin sheets. Once again that can only be found in specialty food establishments. We were able to find a brand made in Germany, Oetker. Fortunately on the packaging they indicate that one sheet of gelatin is the equivalent of approximately ⅙ of a packet of unflavored, granulated gelatin.

18. Almost all of the recipes call for lemon zest. Avoid including the white pith underneath the yellow zest of the lemon. A wonderful new tool for zesting is the rasp.

19. Confectioner's sugar and powdered sugar are synonymous.

20. In most of the recipes, we cook mixtures that contain eggs. In those cases it is always important to keep stirring to insure the eggs do not solidify and scramble. In a round bottom pot, a wisk will do quite well. But in a flat bottomed pot, it may not mix well in the bottom corners of the pot. In that case you might do better using a wooden spoon for stirring.

Les Ambassadeurs at the Hotel Crillon

There are so many locations in Paris that are visually stunning, that it is difficult to select one as being more outstanding than the others. But for those who know Paris well, the view at Place de Concorde from the Crillon side, looking across the Concorde bridge (Pont de la Concorde) to the National Assembly Building and Invalides, is almost impossible to surpass. At night, when it is all lit up, it is particularly breathtaking. Beyond it, and to the right, rising high into the sky, and lit beautifully, is the Eiffel Tower. With all the traffic, foot and auto, dashing madly about, it is an absolutely delicious sight.

But it was not always so. The building of the bridge to honor King Louis XV started in 1755 and ended in 1775. Then in 1793 it became the place where the guillotine was set up which beheaded more than thirteen hundred French men and women, including Marie Antoinette, Mme. du Barry, Robespierre and the Girondins. Two years passed before the blood bath ceased.

A short Metro ride took us to the Place de Concorde stop. We walked along the Rue de Rivoli in front of the private and very exclusive Automobile Club to reach the Hotel Crillon. Doormen were helping guests either arriving or leaving by

The Crillon Hotel at the Place de Concorde

taxi. Others were there just to turn the revolving doors. God forbid a guest there should even have to use their own power to turn the revolving door.

We entered a luxurious lobby and turned to the left where signs directed us to the Ambassadeur Restaurant.

We entered a huge foyer with high ceilings. Just off to the left there is a harp, apparently used for background music at tea time. The lounge is filled with overstuffed chairs and sofas; four beautiful chandeliers hang from the ceiling. A glass case holding the "elephant liquor cave" replica stands in the center. In its original form it had a prominent position at the Bastille, ordered by Napoleon, in 1808. Made by Baccarat, it is a glass elephant with a gold saddle across its back holding multiple bottles of liquor. In one corner of this sumptuous room there is a Grand piano.

At the far side of this lovely lounge there is a bar and large glass doors which lead to the restaurant. The moderate sized room houses about twenty widely spaced tables for dining. A series of glorious chandeliers lines the center of the room, with crystal sconces on the walls. The ceiling has beautiful carvings that appear to be gargoyles on the wooden moldings. The walls are all done in marble.

"We are Madame and Monsieur Keyser, here for lunch and an interview about the tarte au citron."

"Oh yes! The tarte au citron!"

We were obviously expected.

On this particular search we had been accompanied by one of our children, which made our introduction to the restaurant even easier. Our son was actually a guest at the Crillon for several days, doing promotional interviews about his television show which was being seen in France. Earlier that day the staff had seen him surrounded by television cameras and multiple TV and print media interviewers.

The superb meal started with the typical small "cadeau" or surprise, customary in the finest restaurants in Paris. In this particular case it was a small pastry shell stuffed with a meat mixture. A second unexpected item was melon and Parma ham in beef jelly. Both of these were quite delicious.

For her appetizer Barbara had leeks prepared in a loaflike bundle with each portion served as a slice of the loaf so that the leeks were in a cross section in their presentation. My appetizer was a wonderful risotto. Our main course was the seafood sausage with mussels on the side and spinach quenelles.

Once we were ready for dessert we were greeted by two individuals, Karin Graham-Wood and the patissier, Christophe Felder. Madame Wood was a charming woman who spoke perfect English, of course! She was in charge of guest relations and was to serve as the interpreter for the tall handsome young man, the master patissier of Les Ambassadeurs Restaurant.

Christophe Felder has been at the twenty year old restaurant for the past nine years. Christophe, who is from Strasbourg, considers his recipe for tarte au citron to be more typically Alsatian. He prepares tarte au citron every day and although he makes sufficient lemon cream and almond cream to last for several days, he prefers to make his pastry fresh every day rather than freezing it.

Christophe told us there are many ways to make this dish. Although some patissiers bake it after the lemon cream has been placed in the pastry shell, he still prefers both the pastry and the cream cooked separately. He told us that baking them together changes the flavor of the lemon.

For the restaurant he also makes the very small finger size tartes that are served on a platter with several other pastries called mignardise at the end of every guest's meal. When he makes these small tartes he excludes the almond paste.

Cristophe Felder

Christophe, for special occasions makes a large number in advance and freezes the entire completed tarte. In that recipe he finds he must use margarine rather than butter, and because of that he does not prefer it.

His recipe is in the Alsatian style but he varied it by adding more butter. Christophe told us regional variations are innumerable; some use gelatin and some do not. Others even use prepared lemon juice rather than fresh, which he assured us he could never do. None of the fifteen patissiers we worked with on this book used anything but fresh lemon juice. Some even refused to use any lemons other than Menton lemons (a specific French lemon) for their recipe. Christophe told us that one of the variations he dislikes is adding meringue to the top. It is interesting here to note that although we made no request of any of our patissiers to use or not use meringue, only one of our fourteen recipes has a meringue topping.

When asked about his personal feelings, Christophe told us the tarte was a dessert he liked very much, but then added, "I love all sweets".

The combination of a wonderful meal in a beautiful setting, a delicious dessert treat, being joined by our son and the company of a charming patissier made this visit a very special event. Christophe asked about our home kitchen and cooking experiences, saying that he would love to come to San Antonio and make one of these tartes for us in our kitchen. However, with the hectic schedule he has at Les Ambassadeurs Restaurant in the Crillon Hotel, we will not hold our breath waiting for his arrival. All that notwithstanding, we would certainly relish such a wonderful visit.

TARTE AU CITRON

See color photos on page 52

Please read the chapter on Helpful Hints
before starting this recipe

SWEET VANILLA PASTRY INGREDIENTS
(This volume is sufficient to make two 7–9 inch tarts)

Softened Butter at room temperature	⅔ cup
Confectioner's sugar	1 cup
Almond Powder	⅓ cup
Salt	Pinch
Large whole eggs	1
Vanilla	¼ tsp.
Sifted Flour	2 cups

This recipe can be made two ways. This was one of the recipes in which the patissier made the pastry completely by hand. Monsieur Felder adds together by hand all the ingredients in the center of a circle of flour on a marble slab. Then gently by hand adds the flour into the mixture. He smoothes the pastry and then briefly places it in a mixer, using the hook. This technique can be used but may be more difficult for those who are inexperienced in handling pastry. In all these recipes the least amount of handling possible is important in preparing the pastry. However, we were able to make the same recipe using only a food processor.

1. Before starting, soften butter and measure out all the ingredients.

2. Add all the ingredients into the food processor with the flat metal blade.

3. Pulse the processor in many short pulses of a second or two, until a ball of dough is formed. Divide the ball in two approximately equal portions and shape them into discs for easier preparation when rolling out the dough.

4. Wrap each portion of the dough in plastic and refrigerate for a minimum of two hours. See Helpful Hints #'s 10 and 12.

WHEN READY TO PREPARE YOUR TARTE:

1. Preheat the oven to 375 degrees. (This generally should be done about 30 minutes in advance of baking.)

2. Butter well the inside of an 7–9 inch baking rim and place it on an unbuttered cookie sheet.

3. Remove the pastry from the refrigerator and quickly roll it out on a cool surface to a thickness of approximately ⅛ of an inch. Roll it large enough so that it will extend an inch or two on all sides greater than the size of the rim.

4. Drop the pastry gently over the rim allowing it to fall through the rim, down onto the cookie sheet.

5. Fold the excess back against the inside of the rim to double the thickness of the sides of the tart.

6. With a very sharp knife, slice off the excess above the top of the rim. AND MAKE FORK HOLES IN THE BOTTOM OF THE PASTRY OR IT WILL BULGE UP IN BAKING.

7. Place the cookie sheet with rim into the oven for about seven minutes and remove. You will find that the dough on the sides of the rim has begun to slip down. With a teaspoon re-press the dough up against the side of the rim and put back into the oven for about eight more minutes. Recheck the pastry. The finishing point will be when the pastry begins to turn a light golden brown. Check it frequently. Taking it out too soon will make the tart doughy and underdone. Leaving it in too long will result in too hard a crust.

8. While the pastry is baking, prepare the almond cream.

9. When golden brown, remove the pastry from the oven and place on a cooling rack.

ALMOND CREAM INGREDIENTS

Large whole egg	1
Almond Powder	½ cup
Granulated Sugar	5 Tbsps.
Softened Butter	¼ cup
Dark Rum	1 tsp.

1. Before starting, soften butter to room temperature and measure out all the ingredients.

2. Mix all the ingredients well in a mixer.

3. Apply the cream onto the baked pastry with a pastry brush.

4. Return the pastry to the oven and bake for an addition two minutes.

5. Remove the pastry from the oven and place on a cooling rack.

(When Almond powder is not available I have made this recipe without the almond cream)

LEMON CREAM INGREDIENTS
(This mixture is sufficient to make the filling for one tart only)

Granulated sugar	½ cup and 1 tsp.
Large whole eggs	2
Lemon juice	¼ cup plus three Tbsps.
The zest of two lemons	
Butter	½ cup plus 2 Tbsps. in small pieces
Gelatin sheets	2 (If unavailable use approximately ⅙ packet of unflavored granulated gelatin.)

1. Before starting, prepare lemon zest, soak the gelatin sheets in cool water and measure out all the ingredients.

2. In a saucepan over medium heat combine the sugar, eggs, lemon juice and zest for several minutes until slightly thickened. Stir continuously with a wooden spoon in order to reach the bottom corners of the pot. Do not allow the mixture to get too thick. If cooked too long the eggs will tend to scramble. Small pieces will be removed at a later step by passing it through a strainer.

3. Lower the heat and add the butter and the softened gelatin to the mixture stirring continuously. When thoroughly mixed remove from the flame and mix with an electric mixer for at least one minute.

4. Pour the lemon cream through a strainer into the cooled pastry, filling to near the top. Allow the cream to congeal in the refrigerator before serving.

Relais D'Auteuil

We had lots of plans for this day beside finding a special tarte au citron. We began in an area of the city quite different from where we would ultimately go in our search for the tarte. We took the Metro to the 4th arrondissement to wander through the many shops selling foods of every type on the Rue San Antoine. That very old section of the city is called the Marais.

Most of the shops on that street charge less for their foods than other neighborhoods we have visited. There is great charm to the Marais and it draws its fair share of tourists. Right down the road on Rue San Antoine is the Bastille, with its large monument in the square, commemorating the Revolution, and the beautiful new Bastille Opera House.

There were no tartes au citron that struck our eye. But we did purchase an assortment of foods from different shops for our dinner, an array of marvelous middle-eastern foods. After dropping off our purchases at the apartment, we headed to one of the most luxurious parts of the city, the 16th arrondissement, bordering on the beautiful park, the Bois de Bologne. It was there that we would have our next appointment in our search for the best tarte.

After our restaurant visit, we traveled back to the Champs Elysees to go to the Grand Palais, one of the many great museums in Paris. We had read about the special exposition featuring the famous French photographer, Man Ray, who was a friend of the great painters and intellectuals living in Paris between the two World Wars.

We were somewhat surprised by the large crowd at the Grand Palais. One of the most interesting pieces of information came in the beginning when we read the historical notes about the artist. The famous French photographer Man Ray was actually Emmanuel Ridnitsky of Philadelphia, Pennsylvania. Herb's father was born there around the same time, probably in the same Jewish ghetto.

By the time we left the museum and got home it was well after seven. With a lot of Paris covered today we were quite tired and glad that we had food at the apartment to share for dinner while reading and listening to music in the background.

But nothing during the day could match the surprise we found in our search for the tarte. The restaurant Relais D'Auteuil had been our destination for lunch and a tarte au citron.

We ran into difficulty at the very start of this day when we told our French landlady where we were going.

"Today we will try the tarte in 'Re-lay Doe-teal'" (our phonetic pronunciation).

For that we were severely chastised.

"You cannot go anywhere with your French. It is terrible and no one will understand you."

The tongue lashing was not of a minor nature. We felt as if we should crawl into a hole and remain there until given permission to leave.

"The proper pronunciation is Re-lay Doe-toya. Please learn to speak French a little bit better."

Chastened, we took the Metro to the stop Porte d'Auteuil. When we came up to the street we were in the middle of a beautiful, but gigantic, traffic circle. It took us at least fifteen minutes to figure out the location of the restaurant after several inquiries had led us into the wrong direction.

The restaurant is small, with about fifteen tables, but very charming. By the time we arrived all the tables except ours were already occupied. The hostess was expecting us and very cordial as she led us to our table. The table was set with a bouquet of lovely flowers in the center and beautiful modern service plates. The walls were covered in a yellow and white silk with wainscoting on the lower portion. There were crispy baby baguettes in a basket on the table.

After the small cadeau, a beautifully prepared sardine with pimentos, dill and chives served warm with an olive oil dressing, we each had different entrees. I had a small ring of puffed pastry with rougees (fish) neatly stacked with a wonderful anchovy and basil sauce. Barbara's choice was plump warm oysters wrapped in spinach leaves in a shallot sauce. For the main course we made the same choice, a rack of lamb and a lamb filet in a light brown reduction with thinly sliced carrots. The flavors were exquisite.

When the anxiously awaited dessert arrived it looked like nothing we had seen previously. Quite tall, approximately one and a half inches high, the pastry shell extended well above the lemon portion of the tarte. The plate also held a large clear ribboned tart lemon wafer, a scoop of sorbet and a lightly fried basil leaf projecting from its center. The sorbet which had a very tart lemon flavor contained pieces of the basil. The presentation was beautiful and meeting with the patissier was to be quite a surprise.

"Parlez-vous Anglais?" was our regular first sentence to the chefs, hoping we would be able to communicate in English.

With a strong Scottish brogue he assured us that English was his language of choice.

Restaurant entrance near Bois de Bologne

Kirk Whittle trained in Scotland and has been a pastry chef for twelve years. He left Scotland and worked in Bermuda for three and a half years before spending a year in Melbourne, Australia perfecting his talents. From there it was back to the British Isles where he worked for a year in the Lake District north of London.

Making his way to France, Kirk took a position in a restaurant named Vanel and then at Jean Chiche, a pastry shop in Toulouse. Afterwards, he spent five months at the famous restaurant Michel Trama in Puymirol, before returning to the pastry shop in Toulouse.

Moving to Paris, he worked in the well known restaurant Jacques Cagna before arriving at Relais D'Auteuil where he has now been for two years.

He has very strong feeling about tarte au citron, which he says is the classic and traditional French dessert. His present variation of the tarte is one he has made for about three years. He makes it all year round but prefers to emphasize it in the winter when there is less availability of the other fruits such as berries from which he makes tartes.

For Kirk, freshness is all important. He stores nothing, making everything fresh each day. His usual pattern is to make one large tart for every meal that it is offered. If he were serving it for both lunch and dinner, one would be made in the morning and the dinner tarte would not be made until the afternoon. The recipes he provided, however, do allow for preparation the day before.

TARTE AU CITRON

See color photos on page 53

*Please read the chapter on Helpful Hints
before starting this recipe*

THIS DELICIOUS TART IS ONE OF THE MORE DIFFI-
CULT TO MAKE FOR SEVERAL REASONS. ALL OF THE
TARTS THAT ARE CONSTRUCTED WITH THE LEMON
CREAM BEING BAKED WHILE IN THE CRUST ARE
THE MOST DIFFICULT. THIS TART ALSO HAS THE
CHALLENGE OF BEING VERY DEEP. IT IS ABOUT
1½–1¾″ AND PRESENTS PROBLEMS FOR THE
NOVICE IN KEEPING THE SIDES OF THE PASTRY
FROM COLLAPSING DURING THE FIRST PART OF
THE BAKING PROCESS.

THE LEMON CREAM CAN BE MADE THE NIGHT
BEFORE AND REFRIGERATED.

LEMON CREAM INGREDIENTS:
(Sufficient for one 7–9 inch tart)

Large whole eggs	4
Egg yolk	1
Granulated sugar	1 cup
Whipping cream	½ cup
The zest of one lemon	
Lemon juice	½ cup plus 1 Tbsp.

1. Before starting prepare the lemon zest and measure out all the ingredients.

2. Mix the eggs and sugar with a wisk, then add the lemon juice and the zest. Add the cream and mix together very well. Refrigerate until it is time to put it into the pastry.

PASTRY INGREDIENTS:
(Sufficient for one 7–9 inch tart)

Pastry flour	1 ¾ cups
Confectioner's sugar	½ cup plus 3 Tbsps.
Sweet butter	½ cup at room temperature, cut into small pieces
The zest of half a lemon	
The scrapings of the inside of half a vanilla pod or ½ tsp. vanilla extract	
Whole egg	1

The following instructions are those of the patissier. See "Helpful Hints" # 3 for an alternative method of preparing the dough for the pastry shell.

1. Before starting prepare the lemon zest, bring butter to room temperature and cut into pieces, scrape out vanilla pod and measure out all ingredients.

2. At a low speed, mix the sugar and butter until well mixed.

3. In a separate small bowl mix a small amount of the flour with the vanilla bean (or vanilla extract) and add the lemon zest.

4. Add the flour mixture to the butter and sugar mixture.

5. Add the egg.

6. Gradually add the remaining flour, mixing as gently as possible, the less handling the better until it forms into a mass.

7. Wrap the pastry in plastic and refrigerate for at least several hours.

WHEN YOU ARE READY TO PREPARE THE TART:

1. Remove pastry from the refrigerator and immediately roll it out on a cool surface to ⅛ to a ¼ inch thickness, using a little flour on the pastry and the rolling pin when necessary to prevent sticking. Roll it out to several inches larger than the rim on all sides. See "Helpful Hints" #'s 10 and 12.

2. Place a well buttered metal rim approximately 1¼ inches high on a cookie sheet covered with buttered parchment paper. Lay the pastry over the rim so that it falls through. Press the sides up against the rim and allow the excess to fall over the top of the rim. MAKE CERTAIN THERE ARE NO HOLES IN THE PASTRY, especially at the angle where the pastry rises from the cookie sheet up the side of the rim. With a sharp knife cut off any excess dough over the top of the rim. The excess can be used to patch any small holes or cracks in the pastry. NO FORK HOLES ARE MADE IN THE BOTTOM OF THE PASTRY. If there are any defects in the pastry, bottom or sides, your tart will be ruined as the lemon cream, still in its liquid form when added will run right through the pastry.

3. Allow to sit for a few hours. This can be done the night before and left in the refrigerator.

4. Preheat the oven to 375 degrees.

5. When ready to bake, a piece of parchment paper is placed on the inside of the rim covering all the pastry. The inside is then filled to the top with dried beans or weighted metal beads.

6. Bake the pastry for 10 minutes and remove from the oven. If using the technique described in **HELPFUL HINTS** and utilizing no parchment paper and weights, remove the pastry from the oven after the first five minutes. Gently with the back of a spoon, without creating any holes in the pastry, repress the sagging dough back up against the sides of the rim and return the pastry to the oven to complete the ten minutes.

7. Remove the beans and the parchment paper from the inside of the pastry and place the pastry back into the oven for at least another 12 minutes or until the pastry is lightly browned. If not using the weights, the pastry can be repressed against the sides of the rim at the ten minute mark before returning the pastry for these second twelve minutes or until lightly browned.

8. Remove from the oven and lower the oven temperature to 300 degrees.

9. With the pastry still hot place the lemon cream into the pastry no higher than ½ inch below the top of the rim.

10. Bake again, with the filled pastry, for another 20–25 minutes or longer until the cream, is no longer liquid.

11. Remove the tarte from the oven and place in on a rack to cool for at least one hour.

12. Remove rim and slice the tarte with a very sharp knife into portions.

If a hand flame burner is available, immediately before serving dust the surface with powdered sugar and singe the surface of the cream very quickly until the sugar caramelizes; serve immediately.

Alternatively, after the surface is dusted with powdered sugar, it can be placed under a broiler, watched very carefully for a very brief time (seconds) until the top is barely singed.

This tarte was quite different from others we tasted; the flavor was absolutely wonderful. It was more tart and served warm. Barbara kept mumbling, "This may be the best! This may be the best". But in all truth she said that after many of them.

The lemon wafers were made with a special technique our non-French host patissier had developed and was keeping a secret. They were extremely tart and offered a wonderful addition in that they took away some of the tartness of the tarte au citron. The lemon sorbet with the basil was delightful.

And we'll never forget the French lesson from our landlady!

La Grande Epicerie–Bon Marché

We walked the streets of Paris all day, never using the Metro, window shopping in the 6th arrondissement, and then headed west toward the Eiffel Tower. There are so many boutiques, restaurants and food shops of every type that it is pure pleasure to wander through those streets. One of the things we commented about during our walk was the problem of choosing what to eat. In Paris every place entices you. A few days in Vienna and Budapest in the middle of our trip to Europe this year found us trying to find food which might be appealing. At times it was difficult. But food is the very heart and soul of French society. The problem in Paris is not finding great food. It is selecting the place you most desire.

We were on our way to the 7th arrondissement. The location, rue de Sevres, is the boundary between the 6th and 7th districts.

Walking toward there we reached rue de Rennes and were overwhelmed by noise of such great volume that people on the street were holding their ears. On rue de Rennes, hundreds of motorcycles, in no formation whatsoever, were barreling down the street, all with their sirens and horns on full blast. We made repeated inquiries about the nature of this mob of motorcycles and motor bikes. No one seemed to know why they were there, who they were, or anything related to this huge throng.

Finally, one cyclist slowed down as people tried to cross the street. A Frenchman standing nearby asked the rider the nature of the event. The cyclist reported that this was a mass demonstration against the passage of a new law which would be restrictive in some way to the motorcyclists. The French are always out on the street either demonstrating or striking.

After the excitement of rue de Rennes we reached Bon Marche for our next stage in search of the best tarte au citron in Paris.

One of the major department stores of Paris, Bon Marche has one entire building devoted to food. It is called the Grand Epicerie and it is well titled, because it is a phenomenal food hall. The displayed foods of every variety, produce, meat, fish, cheese, pastries and wines are absolutely beautiful. There we would try our next tarte au citron.

By the time we were through at the patisserie, and had toured the market, it was time to return to our own neighborhood to get some food shopping done for the apartment. We certainly could have found everything we needed at Bon Marche, but it was a long walk back and we didn't want to carry all our groceries that far.

Our experience at our local market was no less interesting. Those who have been in France know very well that the French bring their dogs everywhere. At Relais D'Auteil, one of the restaurants in this book, a patron nearby had a full size golden retriever by his seat during the entire meal. The dog was so well behaved, we hadn't noticed it until it was time for them to leave.

But, today something happened that beat that by a mile. When we came to the checkout counter of our local market, standing on the cart immediately in front of us was the largest parrot we had ever seen. He was out shopping with his owner. On no leash, he jumped from the cart to the counter onto the moving belt for the checkout of groceries and walked around. His owner gave him some nuts which he shelled with great finesse. He came over to sniff out the products we were purchasing, then jumped up on his owner's hand and left the super market for their next stop. Believe me, it was weird!

After a brief rest back at the apartment, we were out again. We walked from our apartment in the 6th arrondissement through the 5th arrondissement to the island of Cite in the middle of the Seine. We found our way to Sainte Chappelle for a concert of the English Cathedral Choir of Paris. It is a group of about twenty, some younger than ten, up to one who was probably in his fifties. The sound they made in that cathedral setting was thrilling.

By that time it was almost eleven in the evening and we still hadn't had dinner. As we walked along the Quai of the river Seine we considered trying one of the many restaurants we frequent in Paris and spotted one of our favorites, Bookiniste. At that hour we got the only table still available.

It was almost one A.M. by the time we wandered back to our apartment. The activity on our street was in full blast. Hundreds of young people were meandering around the square at Odeon. A large number of them wore brightly striped clothes in yellow and orange. They were celebrating a victory in a rugby match played earlier that evening.

It was a wonderful day in Paris. The weather was grand. We had walked miles and experienced all sorts of wonderful things in this wonderful city. But the most important thing we had done today was meet the pastry chef at Bon Marche and learn about his recipe for tarte au citron.

The pastry chef for La Grande Epicerie is Nicolas Boussin. He is twenty three years old and married. He's only been there for two months so the recipe for their tarte au citron is a new one. He spent five years as the patissier at the Divonne Casino near Geneva. Nicolas told us it is one of the largest gambling casino resorts in the world. While there, in 1994, as patissier, Boussin won the dessert championship for all of France. His submission was a mousseline of chestnuts, rice, chocolate and quince.

Tarte au citron has been a traditional dessert he has made since first becoming a patissier. As the years passed Boussin felt that the dish was too heavy and began changing the standard recipe to suit his tastes. He decreased the quantities both of butter and sugar. The other thing he insisted upon was that the lemon juice must always be freshly squeezed.

Each day he makes at least a dozen tartes. That number increases to about twenty on Saturdays.

In response to the question we asked every patissier, he told us that he has no favorite dessert. He loves them all.

TARTE AU CITRON

See color photos on page 54

*Please read the chapter on Helpful Hints
before starting this recipe*

LEMON CREAM INGREDIENTS
(Sufficient for two 7 to 9 inch tartes)

Lemon juice	¾ cup plus 2 Tbsp.
Lemon zest	Zest of three washed lemons
Large whole eggs	6
Egg Yolks	1 ½ egg yolks (½ yolk is approximate)
Unsalted butter at room temperature	¾ cup plus 3 Tbsps.
Granulated sugar	1 ½ cups
Gelatin sheets (Feuille de gelatin)	2 (or ⅓ packet of unflavored granulated gelatin.)

(Gelatin sheets can be difficult to find but they are available at finer food stores.)

1. Before starting, prepare the lemon zest, soak the gelatin in cool water to soften it and measure out all ingredients.

2. Cook the juice and zest just to boiling and remove from heat.

3. Mix the eggs and sugar in an electric mixer until smooth and then stir into the juice mixture.

4. Cook over a medium flame with the mixture just simmering for five minutes stirring continuously. I have found that stirring with a wooden spoon is better than using a wisk for this purpose. It is difficult to get into the bottom angles of a pot with a wisk which leaves a greater possibility of some egg congealing.

5. Remove the lemon mixture from the flame and add the butter in small pieces and the softened gelatin while continuously stirring until both dissolve. As the mixture cools mix it every five minutes to prevent separation.

6. When it is cool, pass the entire mixture through a fine strainer into a bowl. Cover the top of the lemon cream with plastic wrap directly on its surface and refrigerate.

PASTRY INGREDIENTS
(Sufficient for two 7 to 9 inch tarts)

Unsalted Butter	7 Tbsps.
Powdered sugar	7 Tbsps.
Almond powder	6 Tbsps. (May be omitted if difficult to obtain).
Vanilla bean	Inside scrapings of ½ one bean or ¼ tsp. of vanilla extract
Large whole egg	1
Salt	Pinch
Pastry Flour	2 cups
Cold water	1 Tbsp.

The following instructions are those of the patissier. See "Helpful Hints" # 3 for an alternative method of preparing the dough for the pastry shell.

1. Before starting, scrape out vanilla pod and measure out all the ingredients.

2. In a mixer combine the butter, sugar, almond powder, vanilla and eggs.

3. Add the flour in small quantities with the mixer at a slow speed, preferably using the paddle, until it forms into a lump.

4. Wrap the dough in plastic and refrigerate for at least several hours. It can be done the day before.

WHEN READY TO PREPARE THE TARTE:

1. Preheat the oven to 375 degrees Fahrenheit.

2. Butter well the inside of the pastry rim and place on a buttered cookie sheet.

3. Immediately after removing the pastry from the refrigerator, roll it on a cool surface sprinkling the pastry and rolling pin with flour. Roll to a thickness of ⅛–¼ inch and to a size several inches larger than the rim.

4. Drop the pastry over the rim, allowing it to fall through. Press the pastry up against the side of the rim. When Monsieur Boussin makes a small tarte, approximately 4 inches in diameter, he uses a rim that is about ⅔ inch high and rolls the pastry to ⅛ inch. If it is an 8 inch tarte he uses a taller rim, a little more than ¾ of an inch high and rolls the pastry closer to ¼

inch. Our own experience on the larger sized tart revealed that the pastry was of a better consistency if we could keep the thickness closer to ⅛ inch.

5. Line the entire bottom of the pastry rim and sides with parchment paper and cover the tart with beans or weights. Place the cookie sheet and rim, filled with pastry and weights, in the oven, baking for approximately twenty minutes or until the visible edges of the pastry are golden brown. **See "Helpful Hints" #'s 10 and 12.**

6. Remove the pastry from the oven. Take the weights and parchment paper off the cooked pastry and place the cookie sheet on a cooling rack. When sufficiently cool slide the rim onto a flat bottomed plate and then remove the rim from the pastry.

7. After the pastry has been allowed to completely cool, fill it with the lemon cream. Refrigerate. Like all the tartes in this book they are best served shortly after preparation once the cream has had a chance to congeal. Refrigerated they can be kept and served the following day, but are best when freshly prepared.

Bristol

The restaurant Bristol is located in the Hotel Le Bristol on rue Faubourg St. Honore. Like so many of the great restaurants in Paris it makes its home in the 8th arrondisement, about one block away from the Elysees Palace. The entire area has the wonderful feeling of luxury.

Looking at the President's Palace and honor guard standing at attention outside, the multitude of foreign embassies and the exquisite gardens surrounding all these buildings overwhelms you. The American embassy and the British embassy are just down the street on Faubourg St. Honore. A short walk leads to the rue Royale. A right turn brings you to the beautiful Place de la Madeleine with the church of St. Mary Magdalene sitting proudly at its end.

Just in the past year the city of Paris introduced a new Metro line that ends at the Place de Madeleine. There is barely a place in all of Paris that a person cannot reach by multiple different choices of Metro lines and interlinking between them. For those who prefer to do their traveling above the ground innumerable bus lines lead to every nook and cranny in the city.

If, instead of turning on rue Royale, you continue walking on rue St. Honore for a short distance you arrive at rue de Castiglione where a short left turn brings you to the entrancing

Bristol Hotel across the street from the President's Palace

Place Vendome with its ultra-luxurious jewelry shops and the majestic Ritz Hotel.

If Lasserre was the most formal of the restaurants we visited, the Bristol must absolutely be considered one of the prettiest and most charming. The restaurant is located in a garden room with glass walls on two sides overlooking French gardens. From late Spring to early Fall the restaurant has facilities to serve outdoors.

The room resembles a striped tent with white lattice work against a green backdrop. A hanging fringe from the ceiling matches the green, red and cream colored drapes. There are approximately 20–25 tables and large, four foot high, vases throughout laden with flowers.

The chef at the Bristol is Michel Del Burgo and the patissier is Bertrand Bluy. Bertrand is 26 years old and unmarried. He has been with the Bristol for about three years.

Previously Monsieur Bluy was a chef in Carcassone for two years at La Barbacane. He spent two years in Roanne at Troigros and 8 months as a patissier in Annecy at Biarritz. His is a relatively new recipe for tarte au citron, developed about two years ago.

Though it was difficult to choose anyone of the restaurants in our research as having the best food, we agreed the Bristol was the best meal we had. In all fairness, that day the Bristol was serving a gourmet meal, and of course we tried their special menu.

At the start of the meal three separate surprises were brought to us. First they served a combination of sesame and poppy seed bread sticks. That was followed by eggplant, red peppers and zucchini, very lightly deep fried. Lastly, a carpaccio of salmon with fennel in a cream and oil sauce with chives arrived.

The appetizer looked like a beautiful garden, with multiple zucchinis cut and shaped into flowers. Parsley, sage, rosemary, basil, chives and tarragon flavored a tomato coulis, which sat under artichokes stuffed half with green and half with black olive tapenade. Alongside this savory presentation was a mille feuille filled with herbed cream.

The main course was a rack of lamb with an additional backstrap, It was served on china that had an exquisite blue, yellow and gold pattern on the edge. With the lamb was a melange of scallions, red peppers, garlic and endive in a brown, orange flavored, reduction.

Dessert was served even though our lemon tarte was coming. It was a plate of thinly sliced miniature Victoria pineapples from Guadalupe with a ball of coconut milk ice cream and sesame seed sugar wafers in the center.

A special wine was served with each course.

Three separate platters of mignardise, one with madeleines, the second with chocolates and assorted other candies, and the third with miniature tarts and a chocolate mousse were brought to our table.

Finally, the tarte au citron arrived.

TARTE AU CITRON

See color photos on page 55

*Please read the chapter on Helpful Hints
before starting this recipe*

LEMON CREAM INGREDIENTS
(Sufficient for two tarts)

Lemon Juice	⅜ cup
Lime Juice	⅜ cup
Granulated sugar	1½ cup
Unsalted butter	½ cup plus 2 Tbsps.
Large whole eggs (Mixed)	6
Large egg yolk	1
Gelatin	½ sheet, softened in cool water

(If unavailable, use ⅙ of a packet of unflavored gelatin granules)

1. Before starting, soak the gelatin sheet, if available, in cool water, and measure out all the ingredients.

2. Bring to a boil the lemon juice, lime juice, sugar and butter. Then remove from the flame for two minutes. Then on a low flame add the well whipped eggs while constantly stirring at a simmer for 10 minutes.

3. While stirring over a low flame add the gelatin and continue until it dissolves.

4. Allow the lemon cream to cool for at least twelve hours in the refrigerator.

PATE SUCREE (SWEET PASTRY) INGREDIENTS:

Flour	2 cups
Softened unsalted butter	7 Tbsps.
Granulated sugar	½ cup and 2 Tbsps.
Large whole eggs	2

The following instructions are those of the patissier. See "Helpful Hints" # 3 for an alternative method of preparing the dough for the pastry shell.

1. Before starting, soften the butter at room temperature and measure out all the ingredients.

2. Mix the flour and sugar in an electric mixer at a low speed.

3. Add small pieces of the softened butter and gently work them together.

4. Gradually add in the mixed eggs until you can form a uniform small ball.

5. Wrap the dough in plastic and refrigerate it for at least several hours.

WHEN READY TO PREPARE THE TARTE:

1. Butter the inside of an 7–9 inch pastry rim.

2. Immediately after removing the dough from the refrigerator roll it on a cool surface using a floured rolling pin. Lightly flour the dough to avoid sticking. Roll the pastry to a thickness of ⅛–¼ inch.

3. Roll into a circle several inches larger than the pastry rim.

See "Helpful Hints" #'s 10 and 12.

4. Drop the pastry over the rim, pressing the excess against the sides of the well buttered rim, which is sitting on a well buttered cookie sheet. Make multiple holes with a fork in the bottom of the pastry.

5. With a very sharp knife cut the excess off the top of the rim.

6. Bake for about 15 minutes or until golden brown.

7. Using a pastry bag apply the lemon cream to the pastry shell after it has completely cooled. Monsieur Bluy fills the pastry shell with multiple small mounds of lemon cream so that the surface does not have the smooth flat look of the typical tarte au citron.

8. Finally, on the edge of the filling place paper thin slices of alternating lemons and limes.

Les Celebrites

Les Celebrites is a Michelin starred restaurant that was not previously known to us. The search took us to an unfamiliar part of the city. Exiting from the Metro, it felt like a commercial area, but it was just the direction from which we approached that gave that appearance. We would soon find that we were a stones throw from the Eiffel Tower, an area that we know quite well.

Our map indicated we needed to walk north from our Metro stop toward the Seine. We found ourselves in front of an ultramodern hotel, not the type we have normally been accustomed to in Paris. It was part of the Japanese chain, The Hotel Nikko de Paris.

We entered the lobby and took the elevator up to the restaurant which was sleek and modern and overlooked the Quai along the left bank of the Seine. The look of the Seine from that vantage point is quite different from how it looks in the eastern portion of the city, which is old and beautiful. From the fourth story we could see well toward the east, and appreciate the marked difference in the two areas. Immediately outside our window there was a very modern bridge over the Seine, unlike bridges to the east that are hundreds of years old and very ornate.

Just a short distance up the Quai, along the Seine, is the beautiful complex consisting of the Palace of Chaillot and the Trocadero Gardens, on the Right Bank, and the Eiffel Tower and open green of the Champ de Mars ending at the military college, Ecole Militaire, on the Left Bank of the Seine. That small area has enough going on to keep you busy for some time. But first we would spend a few lovely hours at Les Celebrites seeking another special tarte.

The original chef at this wonderful restaurant was the renowned Joel Robuchon. The present chef was formerly the chef at Tour D'Argent, another very famous Paris restaurant. Les Celebrites itself is very new by Parisien standards, established only twenty five years ago.

The chef patissier is Jean-Louis Cauvin. He is 35 years old, and has been at this restaurant for 18 years. The second patissier is Eric Vallee, who is married and has a three year old daughter. At age 30, he has already spent eleven years at Les Celebrites. Monsieur Vallee was the patissier at the restaurant at the time of our visit. He told us that he trained for his profession at Rennes, a large city not far from Paris.

Not only were the location and the hotel and the restaurant all new to us, the tarte would be as well. This would be the only tarte in our travels which would have a meringue topping, and a very special one at that.

Monsieur Vallee said that their original recipe of tarte au citron had never changed. It was a dessert they did not serve continually, usually about once every two weeks. When they prepare the pastry, unlike some of the other chefs we have met, they find they can keep it refrigerated for about three days, uncooked.

Concurring with almost every other patissier we met in our search, Monsieur Valle believes that tarte au citron is one of the easiest desserts to prepare. He could not identify any one dessert that was his favorite when asked. Like many of the others patissiers he likes almost every dessert.

Before tasting this wonderful tarte au citron a very delicious meal of multiple courses was served. The two of us ordered all different items, sharing each one in order to get the full opportunity to try many dishes. Happily, we passed dessert to get the full pleasure of their tarte au citron.

We were more than surprised when it came out with a meringue topping, the first we had seen in Paris. At first sight we were somewhat disappointed, thinking that this would be more like American lemon meringue pie. Once we tasted it we realized how wrong our first impression had been. This meringue topping not only tasted nothing like what we had experienced in the past, it made for a very interesting balance between its light neutral taste and the tart flavor of the lemon cream.

TARTE AU CITRON

See color photos on page 56

*Please read the chapter on Helpful Hints
before starting this recipe*

SWEET PASTRY INGREDIENTS:
(Sufficient for two 7–9 cm. tarts)

Softened Butter	¾ cup
Additional Butter to butter the equipment	
Confectioner's sugar	1 cup
Salt	Pinch
Eggs	1 large egg mixed
Almond Powder	¼ cup
Flour	2 cups plus 1 Tbsp.

The following instructions are those of the patissier. See "Helpful Hints" # 3 for an alternative method of preparing the dough for the pastry shell.

1. Before starting soften the butter at room temperature and measure out all the ingredients.

2. Mix together all the ingredients, using the wisk at a low speed for the shortest possible time to have them well mixed, adding the flour last.

3. Wrap the ball of dough in plastic and allow to stay in the refrigerator for at least several hours, or overnight, before using.

Bestor Plaza in Chautauqua looking toward the Library

Les Ambassadeurs at the Hotel Crillon

Les Ambassadeurs—Half eaten tart

Very formal dining room

Relais D'Auteuil

Kirk Whittle, Scottish patissier

Tarte with sorbet and "secret recipe clear lemon wafers"

La Grande Epicerie–Bon Marché

Entrance to La Grande Epicerie

Nicolas Boussin

Bertrand Bluy

His beautiful tarte

Eric Vallee

The only tarte with meringue

Fauchon

An individual and full size tarte

Served on a silver tray

The proud patissier Franck Boujeat

The most beautiful presentation

Laurent

Simply, the tarte

Francois Kartheiser

Lecoq

Christian Lecoq

Multiple Tartes

La Marlotte

Only tarte made in a tarte pan

Patrick Duclos

Pierre Mauduit

Mauduit chef

Two slices missing

Gerard Mulot

Exquisite tarte

Gerard Mulot proudly presenting

Michel Rostang

Classy Michel Rostang

Beautiful tarte presentation

Vivarois

Mack Stephan at Vivarois

A very different tarte

Rookie American pastry chef and full-time physician

WHEN READY TO PREPARE TART:

1. Preheat the oven to 375 degrees Fahrenheit.

2. Butter well the inside of a 7 inch pastry rim and the cookie sheet it is sitting on.

3. Roll the pastry to a thickness of ⅛–¼ inch and drop onto the buttered rim. Roll out a sufficient amount to cover the bottom and then be pressed up against the well buttered sides of the rim. See "Helpful Hints" #'s 10 and 12.

4. Remove the excess over the top of the rim with a very sharp knife.

5. With a fork make multiple pricks into the pastry.

6. Bake at 375 degrees Fahrenheit until it becomes golden brown, approximately 13–15 minutes.

7. Remove from the oven and allow to cool on a rack.

LEMON CREAM INGREDIENTS:
(Sufficient for two tarts)

Lemon juice	¾ cup
Granulated sugar	1½ cups
Large Eggs	6
Melted Butter	¾ cup plus 1 Tbsp.

1. Before starting, melt the butter and measure out all the ingredients.

2. Bring to a boil the lemon juice, sugar and butter.

3. Over a low flame, stirring constantly, add the lightly mixed eggs and stop as soon as the mixture thickens.

4. Pass this mixture through a chinoisier (fine strainer) and refrigerate.

5. When the pastry has cooled pour the lemon cream into the pastry and bake again at 375 degrees for 15 minutes.

6. Cool on a rack for a minimum of 2 hours before adding the meringue topping.

COCONUT MERINGUE FOR LEMON TART
(For one tart)

Egg whites	3
Granulated sugar	6 Tbsps.
Confectioner's sugar	¾ cup
Grated unsweetened coconut	3 Tbsps.
Coconut milk	2 Tbsps.

(If it is difficult to obtain the two coconut items, or coconut is not preferred, the meringue can be made without those two ingredients.)

1. Before starting measure out all ingredients.

2. Preheat oven to 475 degrees Fahrenheit.

3. At high speed mix the eggs and sugar to soft peaks.

4. Then fold in the coconut and coconut milk or move on to step 5 if the coconut is not to be used.

5. Using a pastry bag squeeze the meringue onto the surface of the lemon cream in small swirls, like waves on the water.

6. Then place the tarte into the oven at 475 degrees Fahrenheit for just a very short time until the meringue gets slightly singed. Watch closely to avoid burning. This will take only a few minutes. Remove immediately and serve.

This tarte was quite delicious and completely different from any of the others in this book.

Fauchon

No other establishment described in this book, and probably not in the world, can equal the sheer volume of gourmet foods offered by Fauchon. Established in1886 by Auguste Fauchon it is well into its second century of operation. The worldwide operation now has 17,000 items in its offerings, of which 4500 are their own products. With a workforce of 300 people they have 750 sales outlets in thirty two countries.

They offer produce from every corner of the world as well as a selection of 108 types of jam, 31 varieties of honey, more than 100 teas, 44 different mustards, 56 flavors of vinegar, 60 kinds of chocolate and 2500 wines and spirits.

But these numbers alone cannot convey the marvelous feeling one experiences when moving through the multitude of wonderful shops that comprise this complex. Fauchon is nothing less than a gastronomic museum. We never fail to make a stop here when we come to Paris. It is located in the heart of Paris, at the beautiful Place de la Madeleine. We wanted to know what happens behind the scenes in this wonderful establishment whose tarte au citron has been one of our favorites for years.

It was not easy making the arrangements to obtain the recipe for their tarte au citron. Unlike all the other establishments we visited this is a giant business we had to find our way through.

World famous Fauchon at Place de Madeleine

Alice Bouteille, a lovely young French woman, is in charge of their public relations and communications. Through her we sought a personal meeting with Sebastien Gaudard, the chef patissier at Fauchon. He arrived at Fauchon in 1994 at the age of 24. In January of 1997 he achieved his present position there. He stated that his mission is to maintain the creative traditions of the Fauchon name. For him the composition and presentation of his products is an art form.

Sebastien originally trained in his parents' patisserie in Lorraine. He then apprenticed south of Alsace with George Vergne before spending two years with Jacques Mulhouse. He spent time in military service as a patissier as well

Today Chef Gaudard has a staff of 25 making more than 170 cakes, petit fours, ice creams and desserts sold in the shops and served at the brand new Salon de The. The recipe for tarte au citron at Fauchon is now twenty years old, with minor changes made over the years. The staff prepares between 400–500 each week, including large volumes of the pate sucree which can be kept for three days when refrigerated. They prefer to use only Menton lemons, which are available only at certain seasons, for their lemon cream. As a result, when those lemons are available, they will juice them, zest them and freeze the products for later use.

Once prepared, the lemon cream can also be kept refrigerated for up to three days.

Preparing this volume of tartes involves multiple individuals. To obtain uniformity it is necessary for the technique of preparation (specifically cooking temperatures) to be very exact.

Sebastien told us that the tarte au citron is one of the biggest sellers in their repertoire of desserts.

He is still unmarried and has had the opportunity to visit the United States. Having achieved this position at such a young age there is no way of telling where his career will take him.

TARTE AU CITRON

See color photos on page 57

*Please read the chapter on Helpful Hints
before starting this recipe*

PATE SUCREE (PASTRY) INGREDIENTS:
(Sufficient for two tarts)

Unsalted butter softened at room temperature	½ cup and 2 Tbsps.
Salt	Pinch
Vanilla	Scrapings of ½ of a vanilla bean or ½ tsp. of vanilla extract
Confectioner's Sugar	1 cup
Almond powder	¼ cup
Large whole egg	1
Flour	2¼ cups
Cinnamon (Optional)	¼ tsp.

The following instructions are those of the patissier. See "Helpful Hints" # 3 for an alternative method of preparing the dough for the pastry shell.

1. Before starting, soften the butter to room temperature and measure out all ingredients.

2. In an electric mixer add the ingredients one at a time in the order listed.

3. Once the flour has been added mix the ingredients only until the mixture is homogenous. An optional addition to the pate sucree would be ¼ tsp. of cinnamon.

4. Wrap the ball of dough in plastic and refrigerate for at least three hours.

LEMON CREAM INGREDIENTS:
(Sufficient for two tarts)

Zest of two lemons	
Granulated sugar	1 cup
Lemon juice	1 cup
Large whole eggs	4
Unsalted butter	1 cup plus 3 Tbsps.

1. Before starting, soften the butter to room temperature, prepare the lemon zest and measure out all ingredients.

2. Combine the prepared zest with the sugar.

3. Then add to that mixture the juice and the eggs and mix with a wisk.

4. Fill the bottom of a double boiler with water up to just below the top pot. When the water begins boiling put on the upper pot with the mixture and stir while cooking until the mixture thickens.

5. The temperature should reach approximately 180 degrees Fahrenheit. Remove the pot and strain the mixture through a chinoisier (Fine strainer).

IF MEASURING THE TEMPERATURE IS NOT POSSI-
BLE JUST COOK UNTIL THE MIXTURE BEGINS TO
THICKEN.

6. Allow it to cool to 125 degrees, then add the butter in small cubes. As the butter melts, wisk the mixture to make it homogenous.

ONCE AGAIN, IF TEMPERATURE CANNOT BE MEA-
SURED, ADD THE BUTTER AS SOON AS THE MIX-
TURE IS SLIGHTLY COOLED. DO NOT WAIT MORE
THAN 3–4 MINUTES.

7. Refrigerate the lemon mixture for a minimum of three hours.

LEMON CONFIT INGREDIENTS:

Lemon	One
Water	2 cups
Granulated Sugar	3 cups

1. Slice the lemon in paper thin slices.

2. Cook the sugar and water in a pan until it begins boiling. Pour the boiling sugar over the lemon slices in a bowl. Allow to remain standing overnight at room temperature.

WHEN READY TO PREPARE:

1. Preheat the oven to 375 degrees Fahrenheit.

2. Butter the inside of an 7–9 inch tart ring.

3. Immediately after removing the dough from the refrigerator, roll the pastry on a cool surface to a thickness of ⅛–¼ inch, several inches larger than the diameter of the rim. Lightly flour the rolling pin and the pastry.

See "Helpful Hints" #'s 10 and 12.

4. Drop the dough into the tart ring sitting on a buttered cookie sheet. Press the excess dough up against the buttered inside of the rim.

5. With a very sharp knife slice off the excess above the top of the rim.

6. Make holes in the bottom of the pastry with a fork and bake for twenty minutes or until golden brown. If your oven is calibrated high it might take a few minutes less. The best judge will be the golden brown color.

7. While the pastry is baking drain the slices of lemon confit prepared the night before.

ASSEMBLING THE TART:

1. Pour the lemon cream into the baked pastry as high as possible.

2. Apply the drained lemon slices to the surface of the tart.

Additionally one can decorate the top with fresh raspberries.

Lasserre

There was little doubt in our minds that we were in the most formal restaurant in our search for the perfect tarte au citron. Its location is on Avenue Franklin Delano Roosevelt, directly across from the Grand Palais, one of Paris' most important art museums. Most of the very special temporary art exhibitions are held there. During this particular trip we had the great fortune to see the Van Gogh show.

The restaurant with its two Michelin stars overwhelms its patrons with both its setting and the impeccable service. The formal room upstairs has a large central chandelier on a pedestal, much like a giant floor lamp. The room is done in beautiful yellows and blues and 18th century French furnishings. Fresh flowers on railings surround the room.

Servers utilize beautiful antique wood food trolleys with ornamental brass.

Each table displayed a different variety of a sculptured silver bird as its center piece. Each one also had a glass wine decanter with silver trimming in the shape of a duck.

The waiter, concerned that our choices be just right, suggested to Barbara that she change her selections. She had chosen an assortment of three types of terrines followed by the pigeon. He advised her that the two dishes would be too rich together, and recommended that she start with salmon mari-

The Very Elegant Lasserre

nated in anisette, and then have the pigeon. We both appreciate having knowledgeable waiters recommend what they think are the best selections. When we ask for advice it is annoying to have the server say everything is "wonderful".

As usual, the meal began with a surprise. In this case it was a salmon terrine with a cream based sauce on the side. Needless to say, it was delicious.

While Barbara had marinated salmon, I sampled a fish ragout comprised of lobster and assorted other fish. While having our appetizers we watched one of the chefs preparing a main course over a flame on a trolley. As he prepared kidneys in a wine sauce, the center of the ceiling mechanically opened to a bright sunny sky to allow the smoke from the cooking of the kidneys to rise out of the room. In a few moments it was partially closed, leaving about an eighteen inch opening across the room. That would have been the last time we noticed the change were it not for a funny incident. The sunny sky changed and suddenly rain drops were falling on the table of a group of business executives. The remaining opening in the ceiling was immediately shut down.

Barbara's little pigeons were served whole with a wonderful sauce of wild mushrooms. I had rougets with a crustacean sauce.

The time had come for our tarte au citron. The tartes we have found on this search have been uniformly wonderful, including this one at Lasserre. However, there was little doubt that the presentation of this tarte was the most beautiful we had experienced. Served on a silver platter, the tarte was surrounded by cut flowers with thin slices of lemons on the surface of the tarte. The tarte itself looked like a creme brulee as its top had been singed before serving.

Though it looked something like a custard, it was actually quite different. As she tasted it, Barbara said things like, "Isn't it incredible?", and "This is the best one yet!", her oft repeated statement. We both agreed that sprinkling the top with sugar, so that it could be singed, was a great idea.

The patissier, Franck Boujeat, talked with us following the meal. He is thirty years old and had been at Lasserre for just over two years. He is married, with one child.

As we had learned at Laurent, he confirmed the idea that a restaurant patissier should start as a chef. That is exactly what monsieur Boujeat did. Between the two, he prefers to be a patissier.

His career began in Lagny, south of Paris. From there he went to Moscow to become the patissier at Maxim's de Moscou. After a short time he returned to work at several restaurants in France. Those short stays ended with his being named patissier at Maxim's of Paris, where he remained for seven years before coming to Lasserre as patissier in 1997.

He has not changed the recipe we tasted for the past nine years. He corroborated what many other patissiers had told us in that tarte au citron is one of the easiest desserts to make.

When Franck was the patissier at Maxim's, tarte au citron was on the regular menu. It is not at Lasserre, but is added on occasion, depending on the season. While at Maxim's he would make eight tarts every day, each to serve four people. In order to guarantee the ultimate freshness he made them twice a day, four for lunch and four fresh tartes for dinner. The pastry was made every other day in sufficient quantities for two days, but the lemon cream was made fresh every day.

TARTE AU CITRON

See color photos on page 58

*Please read the chapter on Helpful Hints
before starting this recipe*

PATE a TARTE (Sweet Pastry) INGREDIENTS:
(Sufficient for one 7–9 inch tart)

Flour	1 cup
Confectioner's sugar	½ cup
Salt	Pinch
Large whole egg	1 mixed
Butter softened at room temperature	¼ cup plus ½ Tbsp.

The following instructions are those of the patissier. See "Helpful Hints" # 3 for an alternative method of preparing the dough for the pastry shell.

1. Before starting, soften butter to room temperature and measure out all the ingredients.

2. Mix all the ingredients well, either in the mixer with a paddle or by hand, adding the flour last, until you have a uniform smooth ball.

3. Wrap the ball in plastic and refrigerate for at least two hours.

LEMON CREAM INGREDIENTS:
(Sufficient for one 7–9 inch tart)

Lemon Juice	7 Tbsps.
Lemon zest	The zest of 3 lemons obtained with a rape or grater.
Granulated sugar	¾ cup
Whole eggs	3
Oranges	The juice and zest of one orange
Whipping cream	½ cup
Egg yolks	1

1. Before starting, prepare the zest, taking care to avoid the underlying white pith, and measure out all the ingredients.

2. Mix together the eggs, egg yolk and sugar until well blended.

3. Add the whipping cream, the lemon and orange zest and the juice of the oranges and the lemons. Refrigerate.

BOTH THE PASTRY AND THE LEMON CREAM CAN BE MADE THE NIGHT BEFORE AND LEFT IN THE REFRIGERATOR.

WHEN READY TO PREPARE:

1. Preheat the oven to 400 degrees.

2. Butter well the inside of an 8–9 inch pastry rim.

3. Immediately after removing the dough from the refrigerator roll out the pastry on a cool surface to a thickness of ⅛–¼ of an inch. Lightly flour the dough and the rolling pin to avoid sticking. Roll the pastry to a size several inches larger than the diameter of the rim. See "Helpful Hints" #'s 10 and 12.

4. Drop the rolled out dough over the rim sitting on a cookie sheet covered with unbuttered parchment paper. Press the dough up against the buttered sides of the rim.

5. With a very sharp knife cut off the excess dough over the top of the rim.

6. Do not make holes in the pastry with a fork.

7. Cover the pastry on the bottom and sides with aluminum. Place either rice, dry beans or weights on the aluminum.

8. Bake at 400 degrees for fifteen minutes.

9. Take the cookie sheet and pastry out of the oven.

10. Lower the oven temperature to 240 degrees Fahrenheit. Leave the oven door open for a few moments to allow the temperature to drop down to that level more quickly.

11. Remove the aluminum and weights and fill the pastry with the lemon cream to the top of the rim.

12. Bake in the oven at just under 240 degrees for approximately forty minutes. The cream should be cooked but still shaking.

IMPORTANT: DO NOT ALLOW THE CREAM TO BOIL.

---

13. Remove from the oven and cool on a rack at room temperature.

14. While still warm, lightly sprinkle powdered sugar over the lemon cream.

15. Quickly place under a salamander or broiler for a few seconds watching constantly until the sugar is just browning and remove.

16. Cool at room temperature for one hour.

17. Place paper thin lemon slices over the tarte and serve.

Laurent

On a small beautifully-treed street that runs parallel to, and just north of the Champs Elysees is the charming restaurant Laurent. With a doorman out front in its driveway, it looks more like the entrance to an exclusive hotel.

We entered into what looked like a small salon with a bar on one side and a circular restaurant opposite it. The restaurant has large windows around its circumference which look out onto gardens with a rural setting. There are approximately twenty tables, widely spaced, providing a wonderful open feeling. Around the circumference are archways and pillars. The furnishings are traditional, with walls in pale yellow, and white silk with wainscoting.

In the center of the salon there is a circular plush banquet where one may wait. The ceiling contains beautifully carved moldings and art works.

The chef at Laurent is Philippe Braun, a 36 year old who has been there for more than eight years. It was at Laurent where we heard a discussion, for the first time, about the making of a restaurant patissier. The lifestyle of a restaurant patissier is quite different from one who runs a patisserie. Generally, a restaurant patissier will have spent his entire career in restaurants, frequently in the earlier stages as a chef.

The Lush Laurent

At Laurent the patissier is Francois Kartheiser. He arrived at Laurent one year before Monsieur Braun. Francois began as an apprentice in Belgium for four years. He then went to restaurant Madame Castaing in Condrieu, as a chef in that two starred restaurant. That was followed by his year as a chef at George Blanc, a three star restaurant in Vonnas. Following that he assumed his first duties as a patissier at the Metropole in Geneva, where he spent two years. He returned to the position of chef, first at Jean Paul Lacomb in Lyon, then Restaurant Julienne in Toronto, outside Paris. From there he went to a restaurant in Cannes, and finally another in Megeve. All that experience brought him ultimately to Laurent, as the patissier, almost a decade ago.

Francois told us that tarte au citron was one of the easier desserts to create. He has been using his present recipe for approximately three years. Though he likes the dessert a lot,

Francois said he has refrained from eating it due to his personal need to avoid foods with too much acidity.

In his private life, Francois has one daughter, and when we met him he was about to be married to Joel Robuchon's daughter.

After lunch we walked across the Champs Elysees. It is always filled with thousands of tourists who are enjoying the sheer beauty of that thoroughfare. It is lined for most of its length with trees and gardens to the Arch de Triomphe where theatres, shops and restaurants become the prominent tourist attractions. We crossed the Seine at Place de Concorde and walked down Boulevard St. Germaine to a very special church, St. Germaine des Pres, where we listened to one of the wonderful concerts held in churches in Paris.

TARTE AU CITRON

See color photos on page 59

SWEET PASTRY INGREDIENTS:
(Sufficient for two 7–9 inch tarts)

Flour	2 cups
Sweet Butter	7 Tbsps. at room temperature.
Granulated Sugar	½ cup
Salt	Pinch
Large whole egg	One

The following instructions are those of the patissier. See "Helpful Hints" # 3 for an alternative method of preparing the dough for the pastry shell.

1. Before starting, soften the butter at room temperature and measure out all the ingredients.

2. In a mixer combine the butter, sugar and salt and beat until light and fluffy.

3. Add, in alternating portions, the flour and the lightly mixed egg, until completely mixed.

4. Mix together only until it forms into a ball.

5. Wrap the dough in plastic and refrigerate overnight. THE PASTRY CAN BE KEPT REFRIGERATED, ESPECIALLY IF MADE IN LARGER QUANTITIES, FOR UP TO ONE WEEK. (But, Francois makes it fresh twice daily.)

LEMON CUSTARD INGREDIENTS:
(Sufficient for two 7–9 inch tarts)

Egg yolks	4
Large whole eggs	2
Confectioner's sugar	2 cups
Lemon Juice	½ cup
Melted Sweet Butter	5 Tbsps.
Zest of one lemon	

1. Before starting, prepare the zest, melt the butter and measure out all the ingredients.

2. With a wisk mix together the egg yolks, eggs and confectioner's sugar.

3. Add the lemon juice and pass the entire mixture through a fine strainer.

4. Add the melted butter and lemon zest and keep uncooked in the refrigerator.

WHEN READY TO PREPARE:

1. Preheat the oven to 375 degrees.

2. Immediately after removing the dough from the refrigerator, roll out the pastry on a cool surface to a thickness of ⅛–¼ of an inch.

3. Lightly flour the dough and the rolling pin to avoid sticking.

4. Roll it to a size several inches larger than the diameter of the tarte rim and drop it over an 8–9 inch tarte rim, well buttered on the inside, which is seated on an unbuttered cookie sheet. See "Helpful Hints" #'s 10 and 12.

5. Press the excess dough up against the inside of the rim.

6. Making no holes in the pastry, nor weighting with beans or weights, bake the pastry at 375 degrees Fahrenheit for 20 minutes or until lightly browned and remove from the oven.

7. Lower the oven temperature to 300 degrees Fahrenheit.

8. Fill the shell with the custard up to about ¼ of an inch below the top of the sides of the pastry and return to the oven for 25–30 minutes.

9. Turn off the oven and leave the tarte in for another 10 minutes or until the custard becomes firm.

If you have lemon curd confit it can be sprinkled on top before serving. A recipe can be found in the chapter Fauchon. The restaurant uses a commercial preparation.

Lecoq

Not all of the special places for tarte au citron are found among the most popular tourist locations of the city. Lecoq, one of the great pastry shops of Paris, is located in an area much less frequented by tourists. It is in the 15th arrondissement, which borders the Seine, just a short walk from the Eiffel Tower. It is a modest shop in the midst of a bustling residential neighborhood on the busy rue St. Charles.

Christian Lecoq, the proprietor, is an extremely friendly and charming individual. There is no questioning his commitment to quality in the preparation of his pastries, candies and other wonderful goodies in his shop. He converses with great enthusiasm when discussing the proper way to make his products. Christian, who looks younger than his 45 years, began working as a patissier fifteen years ago. The shop was opened by his father in 1960.

Christian displays the numerous honors bestowed on the shop at the entrance. These include the Confederation Nationale of Patissiers- Confissiers- Glacier, Les Toques Chaudes and La Restauration Patissiere.

Lecoq's recipe for tarte au citron has not changed for twenty years. In the shop they sell primarily small tarts, but also make large ones to order. They make ten tartes a day, and

A very busy shop

if any are unsold they give them away. He insists on making them fresh every day.

Christian has three assistants and four apprentices making pastries, ice creams and chocolates. Apprentices stay for two years and then go on to another shop. Christian says it will take an apprentice eight to ten years of training to be considered a patissier.

Christian goes to the market and tastes all the ingredients he will be using before purchasing them. Among the most important is the butter. The quality of ingredients, for him, is vital. He also finds that the best lemons can be obtained in January and February.

Christian is married and has two children. One, a son, is studying to be a patissier like his father. Presently he is training in another shop. I guess that makes for less conflict, like not teaching your own children how to drive a car.

TARTE AU CITRON

See color photos on page 60

*Please read the chapter on Helpful Hints
before starting this recipe*

PASTRY INGREDIENTS:
(Sufficient to make two 7–9 inch tarts)

Unsalted butter (slightly softened at room temperature)	7 Tbsps.
Confectioner's sugar	7 Tbsps.
Mixture of almond powder and confectioner's sugar.	3 Tbsps. and 1 tsp. of each
First pastry flour	½ cup
Large whole egg	1
Egg yolk	1
Pinch of salt	
Second pastry flour	1 ¼ cups

THE PASTRY CAN BE PREPARED THE NIGHT BEFORE.

The following instructions are those of the patissier. See "Helpful Hints" # 3 for an alternative method of preparing the dough for the pastry shell.

1. Before starting, soften the butter at room temperature and measure out all the ingredients.

2. Cream the butter, sugar and the sugar-almond powder mixture in an electric mixer at medium speed.

3. At a low speed mix in the first flour.

4. Add the egg, egg yolk and salt, followed by the second flour. Mix just until the pastry is forming into a ball.

5. Wrap the ball of dough in plastic and place it in the refrigerator for a minimum of two hours. It is fine to leave it refrigerated overnight.

LEMON CUSTARD INGREDIENTS:
(Sufficient for one 7–9 inch tart)

The zest of one lemon

(The best part of the zest according to Christian Lecoq is at the ends of the lemons.)

Lemon juice	½ cup
Unsalted butter	⅓ cup
Large whole eggs	2
Egg yolks	2
Granulated sugar	½ cup and 2 Tbsps.

1. Before starting, prepare the zest and measure out all the ingredients.

2. Mix the sugar and the eggs until pale yellow.

3. In a sauce pan combine the zest, juice and butter and bring to a boil.

4. When the juice mixture has reached boiling, lower the temperature to medium and add the sugar and egg mixture,

continuously mixing slowly with a wooden spoon until the mixture is thick. Do not mix too rapidly to avoid introducing air to the mixture.

5. Transfer the cream to a glass bowl. Once it has cooled, cover the lemon mixture with plastic placed directly on its surface. It can then be refrigerated.

WHEN READY TO PREPARE:

1. Preheat the oven to 375 degrees.

2. Immediately after removing the dough from the refrigerator, roll the pastry on cool surface to a thickness of about ⅛ of an inch.

3. Lightly flour the dough and the rolling pin to avoid sticking.

4. Roll out the pastry to several inches larger than the pastry rim.

5. Butter the inside of an 8 inch pastry rim placed on a cookie sheet covered with a piece of parchment paper, buttered. See "Helpful Hints" #'s 10 and 12.

6. Drop the rolled out pastry through the rim allowing it to sit on the covered cookie sheet and then press the pastry up against the inside of the buttered rim.

7. With a very sharp knife slid along the top of the rim, cut off the excess pastry.

8. With a fork, make holes in the bottom of the tart and bake for 18 minutes or until the pastry begins to turn golden brown.

9. Remove from the oven and allow the pastry to cool.

10. Lift the rim off the pastry and with a spatula fill the pastry shell with the lemon cream, smoothing it out with the spatula to the level of the top of the pastry.

11. If available, an apricot glaze can be lightly brushed across the top of the tart. Then serve.

La Marlotte

The choice of La Marlotte was completely out of the pattern of most of the other restaurants or patisseries in this selection. All the restaurants were rated as the top establishments in all of Paris. All had received Michelin stars. That was not the case for La Marlotte.

Though Michelin lists La Marlotte in its books of recommended restaurants, it has no stars. It lacks the ambiance expected of starred restaurants. La Marlotte is a charming establishment on one of our favorite streets in Paris, Cherche Midi. Located at the western end of the very busy 6th arrondisement, it is bursting with wonderful shops.

Among all the shops on this great street is the most famous boulangerie in Paris. A boulangerie differs from a patisserie in that it primarily makes bread rather than sweets. Most patisseries carry some bread, just as a boulangerie carries some sweets. This special place is Poilane, where the bread is so wonderful that many Parisien restaurants as well as food stores throughout the city patronize it. We love to stop there to pick up a little something.

At least a half dozen years ago, while we were wandering through the area without any recommendation, we stopped in La Marlotte for dinner. It was an absolute delight. That should not be surprising. For us, one of the most wonderful

La Marlotte on Cherche Midi

things about Paris, in fact about all of France, is the realization that one can eat fine food in a plethora of restaurants with no stars whatsoever.

In the smallest of villages we have stopped, with or without recommendations, and been delighted by meals that were delicious. By contrast in our travels through the United States we have found that trying to find even a decent meal in small towns can be extremely difficult. One trick that has sometimes worked is to stop at a local bank, ask to see a bank officer and instead of opening up an account, ask for a restaurant recommendation.

The Zagat Guide to Parisien restaurants lists almost all our favorite restaurants. The Michelin guide lists many restaurants as "recommended", but with no stars. In the 6th arrondisement, where we always stay, there are terrific restaurants such as La Bastide Odeon and L'Epi Dupin which are listed in both. We never leave Paris without going at least once to Brasserie St. Louis.

Unfortunately, these wonderful restaurants generally do not specialize in Tarte au Citron. But in one case we got lucky.

In searching for the best Tarte we took several different approaches. A year in advance we contacted all the starred restaurants asking if they considered Tarte au Citron as one of their specialties, and selected from those who responded affirmatively.

Another avenue was to search through a large series of books which provided restaurant recommendations in Paris. We were looking specifically for restaurants stating that Tarte au Citron was a specialty of the house. Our search led us to a description of the tarte prepared at La Marlotte which the reviewer never failed to order when visiting the restaurant. The description listed it as the very best that reviewer had ever tasted. That led us to include La Marlotte among our choices.

Interestingly, the tarte at La Marlotte is different from any of the others we included. Just as the restaurant is much simpler than the very glamorous restaurants, the tarte itself is quite simple and might be categorized as a country or bistro type.

Obtaining the recipe was difficult. Like the differences between La Marlotte and starred restaurants, the kitchens also differ. La Marlotte has no large staff with chefs, sous chefs, patissiers. The owner, the chef, and the patissier are all the same person. Like many of the small non-starred restaurants, the operation is a family one with just a few employees.

There was no way that the chef could spend any time with us during lunch or dinner since he was occupied preparing all the dishes for his customers.

Scheduled meetings with the owner/chef fell through twice before we finally made contact and were able to find out about Patrick Duclos' Tarte au Citron.

Just going to the area those three extra times was a treat. We never came down Cherche Midi without making numerous stops, if just to window shop, including at Poilane.

Upon our arrival, Patrick took us into his kitchen. While starred restaurants have massive kitchens, Patrick works his magic in a small space that could hardly allow for a large staff to move about. Still his kitchen is large compared to some in little restaurants in France where even just one person has no space to move about. In this small space, Patrick has everything he needs, whether it's tucked underneath a cabinet or hanging from the ceiling. He is always ready to proceed with his delights.

At age 14 Patrick Duclos began to apprentice for his profession working in establishments all over France, finally progressing to the level of a chef. Twenty years ago he opened la Marlotte and now, at age 46, he remains here. Patrick told us that he and his wife have no children and that she works at another restaurant.

When we discussed his preferences for desserts Patrick told us that he loves tarte au citron.

TARTE AU CITRON

See color photos on page 61

Please read the chapter on Helpful Hints
before starting this recipe

FIRST PREPARE THE LEMON ZEST WHICH WILL BE USED LATER IN THIS RECIPE. USING ONE LEMON, REMOVE THE ZEST WITH A MANDOLINE OR A VEGETABLE PEELER IN STRIPS RATHER THAN GRATING. COOK THE ZEST IN WATER UNTIL THE WATER BEGINS TO TURN YELLOW AND THEN STOP IMMEDIATELY AND RUN COLD WATER OVER THE ZEST. PUT THE ZEST ASIDE.

FOR SIMPLIFICATION ONE CAN SKIP THIS STEP AND PREPARE THE ZEST AS IN EVERY OTHER TART AT THE TIME OF PREPARATION.

PATE BRISSE (Pastry) INGREDIENTS:
(Sufficient for two 7–9 inch tarts)

Flour	2 cups
Salt	Pinch
Granulated Sugar	7 Tbsps. plus 1 tsp.
Egg yolks	1
Large whole eggs	2
Butter at room temperature	6 Tbsps.

1. Before starting, soften the butter to room temperature and measure out all the ingredients.

The following instructions are those of the patissier. See "Helpful Hints" # 3 for an alternative method of preparing the dough for the pastry shell.

2. Combine all the ingredients in a mixer, adding the flour last. Mix at medium speed for the least amount of time, just until it begins to form a ball, wrap in plastic and refrigerate overnight.

WHEN READY TO PREPARE THE TARTE:

1. Preheat the oven to 375 degrees.

2. Roll out the pastry to a thin layer approximately an eight of an inch in thickness pressing it down into a teflon coated tart pan with a removable bottom, then double the thickness of the pastry to ¼ of an inch on the upright portion against the rim, cutting off the excess above the top of the rim by sliding a very sharp knife along its edge. THIS IS THE ONLY TARTE IN THIS BOOK MADE IN A TARTE PAN RATHER THAN WITH A TARTE RIM. AS AN ALTERNATIVE IT CAN BE PREPARED WITH A TARTE RIM.

3. Make fork holes in the pastry, then place the tarte pan in the oven with a sheet of aluminum foil resting on its top for ten minutes. See "Helpful Hints" #'s 10 and 12.

4. Remove the pastry from the oven and take off the aluminum sheet. When the pastry is slightly cooled repress the pastry against the side of the rim. Then return the pan to the oven at the same temperature for approximately 10–15 min-

utes, removing it from the oven when the pastry turns light brown.

5. Place on a cooling rack.

LEMON CREAM INGREDIENTS:
(Sufficient for two 7–9 inch tarts)

Large whole Eggs	6
Lemon Juice	¾ cup
Zest of one lemon	

—If not previously prepared as in directions in box at beginning of recipe, do it now on a rape.

Melted butter	¾ cup plus 1 Tbsp.

—I couldn't help but marvel as I watched Patrick Duclos make his tarte. He took out a large block of butter and simply cut off a piece and placed it on his scale where it registered exactly at 250 grams, the exact amount for this recipe.

Granulated sugar	¾ cup plus 3 Tbsps.

1. Before starting, prepare the zest as described in the beginning of this recipe and measure out all the ingredient.

2. Mix the eggs and sugar.

3. Then add the lemon juice, strips of zest and melted butter. Monsieur Duclos cooks the mixture in a copper pot (We cooked ours in a non-reactive saucepan) over a fairly high flame for five minutes, **STIRRING CONSTANTLY**, never allowing the mixture to boil. Remove from the flame as soon as it begins to simmer.

4. By now the pastry has cooled. Remove the pastry from the tart pan by lifting out the removable base and placing the pastry shell on a flat plate.

5. The lemon cream is then strained and refrigerated in a bowl with plastic wrap placed directly on its surface or poured into the cooked pastry almost to the top. Allow it to cool and then serve.

Pierre Mauduit

Of all the places where we might have looked for a special tarte au citron this seemed to be one of the least likely. Our search led us to the 10th arrondissement of Paris. We exited the Metro in an area of the city we had never before seen, and found ourselves in a neighborhood which could not by any stretch of the imagination be called upscale.

We marched down a street of undistinguished stores looking for the shop number for Pierre Mauduit. At last we came to a shop with a lovely window display of pastries, cookies, chocolates and the usual offerings of a fine traiteur (appetizing delicatessen items).

Inside this modest sized shop the cases are filled with eye catching delicacies. Beautiful tartes of all varieties: apple, framboise (raspberry), apricot and flan caught our eye, but particularly the tarte au citron. Individual tartes, the same size as made at almost every patisserie, about three inches in diameter, cost 16 francs, approximately $2.75, in 1999 dollars, or more than twice that price today.

Another case has an assortment of mouth-watering chocolates. Yet another features sorbets in multiple colors, sculptured to represent fruits and other items. Finally, there is a nook where wine can be tasted and purchased. There is even a small espresso bar.

*Front entrance of a small shop . . . with a
giant factory in the back*

Our initial impression was that this was a quaint little shop in the middle of nowhere, but not much more than that. What a mistake!

A distinguished gentleman, Monsieur Odena, the general manager, greeted us. After some brief background information he told us we would meet the head patissier, Alain Bienfait, for the beginning of an amazing experience.

It could be compared to the shock one gets when the opportunity presents itself to go backstage at an opera house. What one finds there is that the stage they have been watching, though it might be quite sizable, is completely insignificant in size when compared to what is behind the scenes.

Behind this little shop is a huge enterprise being run by Monsieur Bienfait. A most charming man, he has spent the last twenty years, though he looks so young it is difficult to believe it, at this patisserie.

The patisserie itself was started twenty five years ago by a patissier trained in Chartre, who subsequently sold it to the present management. There are fourteen people working in that department alone, not counting the employees in the chocolate and traiteur portions of the business. Work begins at four A.M., preparing the many items needed by early morning customers.

We thought that the huge bakery behind the shop was impressive enough until Monsieur Bienfait told us the operation was so large that numerous other outer buildings in the neighborhood are part of the entire establishment. In the days just preceding our visit they had catered parties of up to 1500 people, preparing all of the food.

Monsieur Bienfait told us that they make between twenty and forty large tartes (about the size of a ten inch pie) every day, in addition to a multitude of the small tartes au citron. While we were discussing the tarte au citron, assistants prepared numerous other pastries. One patissier was working in the corner putting chocolate ribbons on top of cakes. Two others were applying whole cherries to the top of another type of pastry.

We then realized that Monsieur Bienfait's plan was not only to give us the recipe, but actually to make a tarte for us, while we were there. It all began when he had one of his assistants bring him the completed pastry base for a tarte. The pastry had been made earlier in the day, and then frozen uncooked. We watched while he demonstrated for us how the pastry was rolled by machine into large sheets. We laughed about the impossibility of having such a convenient machine when preparing tarte au citron at home. He merely pointed to the trusty old rolling pin.

The volume of baked goods produced by this patisserie is so great that everything needs to be highly mechanized in order to yield the necessary quantities. In another part of the patisserie we would later see a machine that could form thirty six brioche in a matter of about 15 seconds. It was very impressive. A separate machine that stamps the pastry for the small lemon tartes cost $50,000. Each separate small tarte is formed in a matter of seconds. It was definitely mind boggling.

Once the mixture for the pastry was completed and rolled out, a round portion was cut out of the pastry, large enough to extend about two to three inches beyond the metal rim used in baking. The dough was then placed over the well-buttered metal rim, and allowed to drop through. Next, the dough was pressed up against the inner buttered side of the rim. Once the sides were well shaped and pressed against the rim, the entire pastry was lightly floured; a rolling pin rolled over the top of the rim cut off the excess dough, leaving a neat shell within the bottomless rim. A fork punched multiple holes into the bottom of the pastry. This prevented it from bubbling up during the baking process. Then it was placed in the freezer. Monsieur Bienfait said that the uncooked shell could remain in the freezer for weeks and even months if necessary. But the turnover at this patisserie probably never allowed it to be more than a few days.

A large batch of the almond cream and the lemon filling had already been prepared. The almond cream was an ingredient of significant importance in their recipe.

Once a tarte au citron is completed, it is refrigerated and either stored for catering or placed in the chiller case in the shop. The obvious question that came up was the shelf life of the tarte, once completed. Monsieur Bienfait said that a tarte made by placing the lemon filling directly in the shell would soon become soggy, as the moisture from the lemon seeped in. As a result, before the filling is put in, a thin layer of almond cream is laid down on the pastry, covering the surface. This acts as a protective shield for the pastry. Over a period of several hours the almond cream itself penetrates the pastry and softens it slightly.

The lemon cream also has a shelf life. If it is not poured into the pastry, we were told it could be kept refrigerated for a week or more with no change in its consistency.

The freshly-made tarte we were eating did not contain almond cream, since we were going to eat it immediately. We also tasted one that had been made previously with the almond cream applied. Both of us agreed, the fresh one had a wonderful crispness, which we preferred to the tarte prepared with almond cream.

The tasting enthralled us, and brought satisfied smiles from Monsieur Bienfait. Though we were certain that the volume of work he had still to accomplish was significant, he insisted on showing us much of the other parts of their operation. We visited the chocolatier and watched three people working together on an assembly line forming hundreds of a particular chocolate delight. We were offered tastes of it, but declined. The number of calories we were consuming in this research was threatening to have a major effect on our body shapes and sizes.

In another area we passed trays of Madeleines just removed from ovens. Without questioning whether we wished to taste them, Monsieur Bienfait thrust one into each of our hands insisting we eat them. We did as we were told and Barbara insisted she had never tasted another to compare with it.

Everything was so enticing, it was difficult to understand how the patissier remained so slim.

TARTE AU CITRON

See color photos on page 62

*Please read the chapter on Helpful Hints
before starting this recipe*

PASTRY SHELL INGREDIENTS:
(Sufficient for two 7–9 cm. tarts)

Butter at room temperature	½ cup
Almond Powder	¼ cup
Confectioner's Sugar	¼ cup
Confectioner's Sugar	½ cup
Large whole egg	1
Egg yolk	1
Flour	2¼ cups

The following instructions are those of the patissier. See "Helpful Hints" # 3 for an alternative method of preparing the dough for the pastry shell.

1. Before starting, bring the butter to room temperature and measure out all the ingredients.

2. Cream the butter with a paddle in an electric mixer until soft.

3. Combine the almond powder and the ¼ cup of powdered sugar and add that mixture to the butter. This process of first mixing equal quantities of the two items, even though more sugar will be used, is called by the French tant pour tant.

4. Then, in the mixer, add the second portion of powdered sugar, the eggs and the flour.

5. Form the pastry into a ball and wrap it in plastic. Place the ball into the refrigerator to cool for at least six hours. Prepare the almond and lemon cream.

ALMOND CREAM INGREDIENTS:

Butter at room temperature	1½ Tbsps.
Almond Powder	3 Tbsps.
Powdered Sugar	1½ Tbsps.
Large whole egg	Approximately ¼ egg
Corn Starch	2 tsps.
Rum	2 tsps.

1. Before starting, bring the butter to room temperature and measure out all the ingredients.

2. Cream the butter with a paddle in an electric mixer until soft.

3. Add the almond powder and powdered sugar.

4. Mix in the egg, corn starch and rum.

5. Place plastic wrap on the very surface of the mixture and refrigerate.

LEMON CREAM INGREDIENTS:
(Sufficient for one 7–9 inch tart)

Zest of one lemon	
Lemon juice	⅜ of a cup
Large whole egg	1
Egg yolk	1
Granulated sugar	⅔ cup
Butter at room temperature	⅔ cup

1. Before starting, bring butter to room temperature, prepare zest and measure out all ingredients.

2. Cook juice and zest until brought to a boil.

3. In a separate bowl mix the sugar and eggs until pale yellow. Add the egg and sugar mixture to the lemon juice and cook again over medium heat, continuously mixing with a wooden spoon not allowing any at the bottom of the pot and in the corners to go unmixed. Remove from the flame immediately as it begins to reach a boil.

4. Then add the butter, still continuously mixing, allowing the butter to melt into the mixture.

5. Strain the mixture through a chinoisier or fine strainer into a bowl and place a sheet of plastic wrap directly on the surface of the mixture.

6. When cool, place in the refrigerator.

WHEN READY TO PREPARE TARTE:

1. After the pastry has been refrigerated for at least six hours you are ready to prepare the tarte au citron.

2. Immediately after removing the dough from the refrigerator roll out the pastry on a cool surface to a thickness of approximately a quarter of an inch. Lightly flour the dough and the rolling pin to avoid sticking.

3. Cut a circle of pastry which extends approximately two to three inches outside the pastry rim. The pastry should reach at least ten inches in diameter.

4. Paint the inside of the rim heavily with melted butter and place it on a cookie sheet covered with parchment paper.

5. Place the round sheet of pastry over the rim and push it down so that the excess can be pressed up against the inside of the rim. When the pastry has been well formed and pressed against the sides take a rolling pin over the top of the rim to slice off the excess dough. **See "Helpful Hints" #'s 10 and 12.**

6. With a fork make multiple holes in the pastry. It can then be frozen or the actual preparation begun.

PREPARING THE TART:

1. Pre-heat the oven to 375 degrees.

2. Bake the pastry in the bottomless rim sitting on a cookie sheet covered with parchment paper in the center of the oven for twenty minutes or until golden brown.

3. Remove the pastry and allow it to completely cool.

4. Apply a layer of the almond cream. This is necessary if the tarte is to be allowed to remain uneaten for more than an hour or so. If the tarte is to be eaten within a short period of time, the almond cream can be omitted and the pastry will be more crisp.

5. The lemon cream is then scooped into the tarte to the surface of the rim. With a large spatula smooth the cream so that it is flattened and slightly higher in the center of the tarte than at the sides. A cardboard circle just smaller than the tarte can be placed under the pastry before slipping off the metal rim.

6. Refrigerate or serve.

At the patisserie each tarte is then coated with an apricot glaze. Its purpose is purely visual as it has no taste. Apricot glaze can be difficult to find for the non-commercial baker. Monsieur Bienfait heated the glaze and then ladled over the tarte allowing the excess to drip off the tart back into the pot of glaze. Some bakeries in the United States are kind enough to sell a small amount of glaze . . . which keeps indefinitely.

Gerard Mulot

This wonderful shop sits on the Left Bank, away from the hum of major streets such as St. Germaine and San Michel and a short distance from the popular Buci market. Here we found a multitude of purveyors of foods of all types. There are supermarkets, a seafood shop, a creamery (cheese shop), bakeries, numerous produce venders, a wine shop as well as restaurants and traiteurs selling "foods to go" of every type imaginable. One shop sells Vietnamese food that we frequently purchased to take home for a meal. Several others have wide selections of beautifully prepared salads and vegetables to take out as well. We tried to eat one simple meal a day back at our apartment, in as much as we were consuming so many large and beautiful meals at the restaurants where we were testing their tartes au citron. It was purely a defensive measure on our part to try to control, to some slight extent, our daily calorie intake.

The streets around St. Germaine, and Buci are constantly bustling with people of all ages, and only a block away is the Odeon Square. The beautiful Theatre Odeon is another block beyond. The corner of St. Germaine is crowded from early morning until the wee hours. There are wonderful restaurants such as L'Epi Dupin and Le Bastide Odeon in the area, as well as four movie complexes. This Left Bank area is always an exciting place to spend time while in Paris.

Entrance to Gerard Mulot on Rue de Seine

The grand pastry shop, Mulot, occupies a quiet corner, but the shop itself is bustling. Customers appear in droves. As many as nine women were serving behind the counters and they moved like demons. Every once in a while one of them would go dashing into the back of the shop to bring out another tray of something else mouth watering. The shop serves a beautiful selection of sandwiches and salads as well as the pastries and chocolates. Everything is done in exquisite taste.

Attempting to schedule a meeting with Monsieur Mulot was not easy. While everyone was cordial, no one spoke English. We all fumbled in each others' language, but finally arrived at a time agreeable for us both. I was thrilled because everything looked so spectacular, the last thing in the world I wanted to happen was to miss this opportunity. I was assured that when the time came for our appointment, Monsieur

Mulot's daughter would be there to interpret. I was thankful because we both needed help desperately.

Monsieur Mulot's language skills were good enough to make a joke. When he noted from my letterhead that I was a physician, he said in French, "I am a gateau (cake) doctor". I could tell right then, from the twinkle in his eye, I was going to enjoy this interview. We set a date. But before we left, Barbara and I purchased an assortment of goodies.

Second Visit

When we returned Monsieur Mulot had not yet arrived, but his daughter who would function as the interpreter was already waiting for us. Florence is 24 years old and extremely charming. We took the time to learn something about our highly respected patissier.

Gerard Mulot grew up in Lorraine where he developed his passion to be a grand patissier. He apprenticed for three years in Lorraine before entering the army. Following his service Gerard Mulot came to Paris to further his training. Three years were spent at the famous patisserie, Dalloyau. In 1972 he officially became a patissier.

His shop gradually enlarged over the years until presently he employs 45 people and four apprentices. Each works in a specific category in the shop, either as a patissier, a chocolatier or a traiteur. But even with all these employees, Gerard Mulot is no hands off employer. His working day varies from 15–18 hours daily, and he loves it.

The recipe Monsieur Mulot uses for his tarte au citron has not changed since he first opened his shop. He told us that he likes tarte au citron very much.

He is especially proud of an award which sits on the counter in the shop. It states, "Best Patissier in all Paris, 1998".

TARTE AU CITRON

See color photos on page 63

Please read the chapter on Helpful Hints
before starting this recipe

PASTRY INGREDIENTS:
(Sufficient for two 7–9 inch tarts)

Butter at room temperature	½ cup plus 3 Tbsps.
Almond powder	½ cup plus 2 Tbsps
Powdered sugar	½ cup plus 2 Tbsps.
Vanilla sugar powder	⅓ ounce

This is a rather difficult item to prepare. The vanilla sugar powder is a preparation that Monsieur Mulot makes himself. He grinds up vanilla beans and combines this with an equal amount of granulated sugar.

IMPORTANT: For the average pastry chef this can be replaced by the scrapings of ½ of a vanilla bean.

Large whole egg	1
Pastry flour	2 cups

The following instructions are those of the patissier. See "Helpful Hints" # 3 for an alternative method of preparing the dough for the pastry shell.

1. Before starting, warm the butter to room temperature and measure out all the ingredients.

2. Combine all the ingredients, except the flour, and mix in an electric mixer until smooth.

3. Add the flour gradually and mix with a dough hook until it is a firm ball. It must be refrigerated for a minimum of two hours before making the tarte. It can definitely be made the day before and refrigerated overnight.

(At the Gerard Mulot patisserie the pastry is made fresh every day. They sell forty to fifty small tartes daily. But, in order that they be very fresh they only prepare ten to fifteen each time and make them several times a day. As for the large tarte, which is what this recipe makes, Monsieur Mulot prepares one or two daily, two every Saturday and three on Sunday.)

LEMON CREAM INGREDIENTS:
(Sufficient for one 7−9 inch tart)

All the zest of one lemon	
Lemon juice	½ cup
Butter at room temperature	½ cup
Granulated sugar	1½ cups divided in two parts
Large whole eggs	2
Egg yolk	1
Maizena (Corn starch)	3 Tbsps.

1. Before starting, soften the butter to room temperature and measure out all the ingredients.

2. Mix the zest, juice, butter and half of the granulated sugar and transfer into a saucepan.

3. Over a medium to high flame bring the mixture to a boil.

4. Strain the mixture through a fine strainer or chinoisier.

5. Allow the mixture to stand and cool.

6. With a wisk or wooden spoon in a saucepan, mix the second half of the sugar, the eggs and the corn starch and cook over a medium heat, whisking constantly, just up to simmering.

7. After removing the egg mixture from the stove, combine the two mixtures and strain again.

8. Put the combined mixture in a glass or ceramic bowl and cover with plastic wrap. The plastic should be placed immediately on the top surface of the mixture.

9. Refrigerate.

(The filling can be kept refrigerated and made the night before or earlier. Monsieur Mulot keeps it refrigerated for up to four days.)

Gerard Mulot uses pastry rims that are approximately 3½ inches in diameter for his small tartes and approximately 7 inches in diameter for the large tarts. The rim is about ¾ inch high in the large tarte.

WHEN READY TO PREPARE:

1. Preheat the oven to 400 degrees.

2. A buttered large rim is placed on a flat cookie sheet covered with parchment paper.

3. Remove the pastry from the refrigerator and roll immediately on a cool surface.

4. Lightly flour the pastry and the rolling pin so as to avoid having the pastry get soft and sticky.

5. The pastry is rolled to a thickness between an $\frac{1}{8}$ to a $\frac{1}{16}$ of an inch. Roll it to a size several inches larger than the diameter of the tart rim. Drop it over the rim allowing it to fall through onto the parchment covered cookie sheet. See "Helpful Hints" #'s 10 and 12.

6. Press the excess up the buttered inside of the tarte rim. Trim off the excess pastry hanging over the top of the rim with a very sharp knife.

7. Parchment paper is placed inside the rim and up the sides and is weighted with metal baking weights, raw rice, dried beans, or in Monsieur Mulot's case, dried out apricot seeds.

8. The cookie sheet and pastry rim filled with weights are left in the oven for twenty minutes.

9. Place the cookie sheet on a cooling rack and remove the parchment paper and weights.

10. When cool, remove the rim carefully and pour the lemon cream into the pastry to just below the top. The tartes can be refrigerated and served at any time.

Michel Rostang

We began this day with a trip to the Musee D'Orsay for a special exhibit of the works of Monet, Manet and other artists who had painted the train station at St. Lazare. As always, the museum was crowded. Transformed from a train station, it is a favorite museum of many.

Afterward we headed for our next try at tarte au citron. We arrived at one of the premier restaurants in all of Paris. The room was absolutely beautiful. The maitre 'd led us through a heavily paneled room to our table, which had settings of beautiful floral patterns with napkin rings to match.

The meal began with a duck pate en croute and a plate of crustaceans on layers of pastry in a sauce. It was as delicious an appetizer as I had tasted in all our meals here. For our main course we both had the special for that day, a lovely pigeon dish. We ordered the sorbet, and an out of this world rhubarb dessert, even though we were still going to have the tarte au citron. It was difficult to limit the amount we ate, even knowing we wanted to save space for the tarte.

At the end of the meal the patissier came out to meet with us and tell us about himself and the recipe. We spent the better part of an hour with him before finally leaving the restaurant. Barbara felt that the tarte was perhaps the best of all those we had tried. But this was not to be the first or last time she would feel that way.

After lunch we walked toward one of our favorite parks in all of Paris, Parc Monceau. One gets the impression that it is not widely known by tourists, who are most frequently sent to the Tuileries or Palais Royale. Like the Tuileries or Palais Royale one can easily cover it on foot. The park has a circular walking path where there are lovely gardens, and a waterway under a small bridge. Children play all over. A section is set aside for roller skating with benches everywhere. It is a wonderful place to visit and a lovely way to complete a day that had begun at a museum, then continued at such a wonderful restaurant for a memorable meal topped off by a very special tarte au citron.

The patissier at Michel Rostang is Stephane Hottlet. This attractive 35 year old man has been at Michel Rostang since 1986, but is expanding out quite a bit on his own. Traveling world wide he has already established a restaurant in Rio de Janeiro and does gastronomic weeks throughout the world including Japan.

Hottlet began his work at the Hotel Frantel-Orly in the early eighties where Monsieur Besset of La Couronne was his mentor. From there he spent several years at the Hotel Ritz before coming to Michel Rostang.

The present recipe he utilizes for tarte au citron is one which he has developed after many changes. He has used this recipe for approximately one year. In this particular variation the lemon cream is not cooked after it has been added to the pastry.

He primarily makes his tarte au citron in the winter when he doesn't have the availability of the many fruits and berries that can be used fresh in the summer. In the winter he will make as many as fifteen of the lemon tartes daily. Monsieur

Hottlet told us it was extremely important to him to utilize only lemons which come from Menton because they are slightly less tarte, possibly similar to the American Meyer lemons.

In preparation for the tartes, he will make the pastry and freeze a quantity uncooked for as much as three days. But the lemon cream will always be made fresh on the day it is to be used.

Presently he has two or three assistants working with him making the desserts, and next year he expects to also take in an apprentice from one of the finer schools in France.

Monsieur Hottlet is married, but he and his wife have not yet had any children.

TARTE AU CITRON

See color photos on page 64

*Please read the chapter on Helpful Hints
before starting this recipe*

PATE SUCREE (SWEET PASTRY) INGREDIENTS:
(Sufficient for two 7–9 inch tarts)

Butter	½ cup and 1 Tbsp. at room temperature
Almond Powder	¼ cup
Confectioner's sugar	¼ cup
Granulated sugar	7 Tbsps.
Eggs	1 Large whole egg plus 1 egg white
Flour	2 cups plus 3 Tbsps.

SEE "HELPFUL HINTS" #3

1. Before starting, soften the butter at room temperature and measure out all the ingredients.

2. Combine the butter, both sugars and the almond powder, one ingredient at a time in a mixer.

3. Add the eggs and finally the flour. When they are completely mixed, with the least amount of handling possible, wrap in plastic and place in the refrigerator for at least several hours.

WHEN READY TO PREPARE THE TART:

1. Preheat your oven to 375 degrees Fahrenheit.

2. Butter well the inside of the rim 7–9 inches in diameter and a cookie sheet.

3. Immediately after removing the dough from the refrigerator, roll the pastry on a cool surface to a thickness of ⅛–¼ inch. Roll it to a size several inches larger than the diameter of the rim. Lightly flour the dough and the rolling pin to avoid sticking.

4. When rolled out drop the pastry over the metal rim. The pastry should fill the bottom of the rim sitting on a cookie sheet and up the sides. Press the dough against the side of the rim and remove the excess off the top of the rim with a very sharp knife.

5. Make multiple holes in the bottom of the pastry with a fork.

6. Bake the pastry until it begins to turn light brown, approximately 15 minutes. Begin preparing the lemon cream while the pastry is baking.

7. When the pastry is cooked remove it from the oven, take off the metal rim and allow to cool for at least ten minutes before adding the lemon filling.

LEMON CREAM INGREDIENTS:

Unsalted butter	¾ cup and 2 Tbsps.
Granulated Sugar	1 ¾ cups
Lemon zest	2 lemons
Lemon juice	½ cup plus 2 Tbsps.
Large whole eggs	4

1. Wisk together the eggs and half the sugar until the mixture turns a pale yellow and put aside.

2. Combine the butter, remainder of the sugar, the lemon juice and lemon zest in the top of a double boiler with the water boiling.

3. When thoroughly mixed lower the temperature to medium and add the egg mixture while rapidly wisking **CONTINUOUSLY** until the mixture becomes slightly thickened.

4. Pour the lemon cream into the already cooled pastry and refrigerate. The tarte au citron should remain refrigerated until the lemon cream is well congealed, probably several hours, and then served anytime after that.

Vivarois

We returned to the sixteenth arrondisement once again to search out our next tarte au citron. We sent our original request to the chef, Monsieur Claude Peyrot, but by the time of our arrival he was not well. As a result, Barbara and I spent the afternoon with Madame Peyrot, a wonderful and charming host.

We had decided to make this trip on the RER, a newer subway system than the original Metro. The function of the RER is to take passengers primarily to suburban areas and make only a few stops within the city proper. That is quite different from the Metro we used on a daily basis, which makes stops every few streets.

Vivarois is located not far from one of the RER stops, the Arche de Triomphe. And, our apartment was near another at Boulevard St. Michel.

There is quite a difference in the two underground systems. The RER actually looks a lot more like railroad trains that travel considerable distances. But that is not the only difference. After disembarking from the train, and making our way to the street, we discovered that in order to exit from the station we had to be able to insert our used ticket into a slot for the exit door to open. We had saved only one and were apparently trapped in the station. Fortunately, an employee came by and, recognizing our predicament, allowed us out of the station.

We walked down Avenue Victor Hugo and on our arrival we were greeted by madame Peyrot. She spent quite a bit of time telling us about the restaurant and her husband, who when he was younger and healthier had quite a career.

Claude Peyrot has been a chef and owner of Vivarois for over 32 years. He began his apprenticeship at the very famous restaurant and hotel Ousteau le Baumanier in Les Baux in the south of France. He then went to a three star restaurant in Vienne and followed that in Paris as a chef at the Ritz and at Lucas Carton before opening Vivarois.

At one time the restaurant had reached the level of three stars, but with his illness it became difficult to maintain, and it is presently a two star Michelin establishment.

Madame Peyrot introduced us to their pastry chef Mack Stephan, who is 29 years old and married to a dental assistant. So far they have no children. He has been with Vivarois for more than three and one half years. Originally from Northern France, he began his work in a two star restaurant in Lille. He has one assistant at the restaurant.

Following our lunch and tasting of the wonderful tarte, we walked down a lovely street, Avenue G. Mandel. Along the way we saw a plaque in memory of the great opera singer Maria Callas.

We continued on to the Trocadero and through the center of the two huge buildings of the Palais de Chaillot. From the elevated positions there one can look directly at the Eiffel Tower and through it to the Parc du Champ de Mare, a spacious green area that extends down to the Ecole Militaire. We walked the entire beautiful area before returning home.

Madame Peyrot had been so nice to us we decided to send her a box of chocolates as a thank you. True to form she wrote us a beautiful note in response.

TARTE AU CITRON

See color photos on page 65

*Please read the chapter on Helpful Hints
before starting this recipe*

PASTRY INGREDIENTS:
(Sufficient for two 7–9 inch tarts)

Flour	2 cups
Butter (Softened at room temperature)	7 Tbsps.
Confectioners sugar	1 cup
Egg	One large
Egg yolks	Two

1. Before starting, bring the butter to room temperature and measure out all the ingredients.

The following instructions are those of the patissier. See "Helpful Hints" # 3 for an alternative method of preparing the dough for the pastry shell.

2. Using a plastic paddle in an electric mixer at a slow speed, mix the softened butter and flour.

3. Add the sugar, and follow with the egg and egg yolks.

4. Form into a ball. Cover with plastic and refrigerate overnight.

WHEN YOU ARE READY TO PREPARE THE TART:

1. Before preparing the lemon cream, prepare the pastry.

2. Preheat the oven to 375 degrees.

3. Immediately after removing the dough from the refrigerator, roll the dough out on a cool surface to a thickness of ⅛ to a ¼ inch.

4. Lightly flour the dough and rolling pin to avoid having the dough get soft and sticky.

5. Roll the pastry to a thickness of ⅛–¼ inch. Roll it to a size several inches larger than the diameter of the tarte rim. See "Helpful Hints" #'s 10 and 12.

6. Lay the pastry over a buttered 7–8 inch tart rim seated on an unbuttered cookie sheet. Allow the pastry to fall through the rim pressing it up against the inside of the rim.

7. Cut off the excess pastry hanging over the rim with a sharp knife.

8. Line the bottom and sides of the pastry with parchment paper and fill the shell with weights or dried beans on top of the parchment.

9. Bake in the oven for ten minutes at 375 degrees.

10. Meanwhile begin preparing the lemon cream and sabayon.

LEMON CREAM INGREDIENTS:
(Sufficient for one 7–9 inch tart)

Butter	7 Tbsps.
Granulated Sugar	½ cup
Lemon Juice	⅓ cup
Lemon Zest	Zest of one and a half lemons on a mandoline or rasp
Egg	One

1. Before starting measure out all ingredients.

2. In an electric mixer combine the egg with the granulated sugar.

3. In a saucepan melt the butter with the lemon juice and zest.

4. Put the lemon juice/butter mixture into the top of a double boiler and add the egg/sugar mixture, heating the combination until simmering. Constantly stirring. Remove from the stove when it begins simmering and thickening.

5. Do not strain to remove the zest.

SABAYON INGREDIENTS:

Large whole egg	One
Egg yolk	One
Granulated sugar	¼ cup
Confectioners sugar	3 Tbsps.

1. Before starting, measure out all ingredients,

2. Whip together the egg and egg yolk.

3. Add the granulated sugar to the eggs and wisk.

4. Gently fold the mixture into the lemon cream which has been removed from the stove.

5. The combination of the sabayon and cream is then folded into the pastry shell which has had the parchment and beans or weights removed, if they have been used. Do not fill the cream/sabayon mixture to the top of the side of the pastry.

6. Sprinkle the top with confectioner's sugar.

7. Bake in the oven at 375 degrees again for approximately ten minutes or until the edge of the crust is lightly brown.

8. It can then be refrigerated or served as soon as it has slightly cooled.